Bot school Tod

Dark Horse

Full Sail

Freubel

OLD SCHOOL, NEW SCHOOL, NO SCHOOL
RE-CALIBRATING HIGHER EDUCATION

OLD SCHOOL
NEW SCHOOL
NO SCHOOL

RE-CALIBRATING
HIGHER EDUCATION

DEBORAH SNYDER, PHD
President, St. Clair County Community College

JOHN DUHRING
Director of Community Relations, Cogswell College

With a Foreword by

JOHN SEELY BROWN
Former Chief Scientist, Xerox
Head of Xerox Palo Alto Research Center (PARC)

Praise For *Old School, New School, No School*

"I am thrilled to see a book that not only articulates the tough challenges inherent in moving from early 19th century academic models to the needs of a 21st century world, but also shine a bright light on the pathway toward what higher education models can and should look like in the next 20 years. The intersection of creative design, business, and technology skills in immersive, real world studio and lab environments is the essence of learning and developing preparation for the jobs of the 21st century. The authors capture the power of project and team based learning as people who have clearly experienced the future first hand and are returning to the present day to lead us toward learning environments and experiences that can change the world for all learners. For those committed to making a difference in the lives of students and our academic communities, following the principles in this book can drive real impact."

—**Scott McKinley**, Amazon Web Service Academy Global Lead,
Co-founder of Neumont University.

"Most schools today still replicate those established in the nineteenth century to prepare factory workers and infantrymen. The world today could not be more different from the conditions that inspired the design of the traditional school. Yet we still lack coherent outlines of what twenty-first century education should look like. Duhring and Snyder admirably fill this gap."

–**Charles MacCormack**, President Emeritus, Save the Children

"As the landscape of education transforms into ubiquitous and accessible, anytime, anywhere knowledge for all, Snyder and Duhring remind us that educational institutions have a special niche as cultures of learning. While colleges of the past were built to produce academics and support publishing houses, new schools can be designed to produce life-long learners and thriving citizens, well prepared to operate in an ecosystem of change."

–**Marcy Delgado**, Hacker Dojo Community Outreach Advisor and
Co-founder of CoderDojo Silicon Valley

Contents

Acknowledgements

This book is the product of many, even if written by a few. The authors feel honored to have met at Cogswell Polytechnical College, which has been described as "a fiercely collaborative living laboratory" with a century-old heritage of "students learning with instruments in their hands". To the faculty, staff and students who have worked and continue to work at Cogswell, this book is about what you have put in place. It forms a blueprint for higher education at a time when technology and cultural forces are changing decisions at academic institutions of every size as well as for families with students in high schools around the world. By embracing "the intersection of creativity and technology", the Cogswellian culture is carried and spread by all who have been fortunate to find their fire and develop their talents there.

The authors also wish to thank some special individuals who have helped us develop our perspectives. After his first visit to Cogswell, John Seely Brown declared, "I don't think you guys realize what you have here"! Since then, the wheels have been put in motion, greatly due to his encouragement. Brewster Kahle, founder of the Internet Archive, has demonstrated by his example the value of "universal access to all human knowledge" and how it can be applied. John Mitchell, Vice-Provost for Teaching and Learning at Stanford, has been invaluable in supporting the notion that we are all in the culture business. Dale Dougherty, founder of MAKE magazine and creator of the Maker Faire, provided us with ample evidence supporting the global possibilities of a new perspective for higher education.

In addition, thanks to the many who have resonated to the message and rallied to the cause. Imran Saddique at investvine. com has been publishing segments through his website while offering invaluable production assistance. Norman Jackson at Lifewide Magazine was helpful in developing the introduction. Gordon Freedman suggested the addition of "No School" to our title. Anne Forte provided masterful edits to the manuscript. Our spouses and family members have patiently supported our efforts even as our path has been far from straight and smooth. For the many we have neglected to mention here, our deepest apologies for any oversight or instances of neglect. All inaccuracies or omissions are exclusively ours.

FOREWORD

John Seely Brown

Advisor to the Provost at the University of Southern California,
Former Head of Xerox Palo Alto Research Center (PARC)

For the last six years my colleague Ann Pendleton-Jullian and I have been writing a five volume opus on Designing for Emergence in a White Water World—a world that is constantly changing, hyper connected, and radically contingent—a world where most of the most problematic issues are deeply entangled with each other. We find ourselves in a new world where public policies can't keep up, where the unintended consequences of new technologies and their assimilation end up swamping the intended results. Said both poetically and forcefully by our good friend, John Rendon—"We are forcing the past as a solution set. But the past as a solution set is no longer a viable option. We need a new tool set."

Although the above thoughts emerged from our work on defense and public policy issues, they evolved as we became more and more engaged in the most urgent challenges and most compelling opportunities around education. We know we need a new framework for educating our kids today and tomorrow. The past as a solution set won't work here, either. Indeed! We need to prepare our students to thrive in a white-water world—to be able to view the constant changes and new kinds of entanglements as opportunities for learning. But these kinds of new learning situations require skills, resolve and a collaborative disposition and drive, all in support of learning as an adventure.

In a world where many of our skills have a half-life of no more than 5 years, we all need to learn in, and through, action of experimentation—action that is best undertaken collaboratively. Collaborative action that is experimental by nature and intent taps into the creative diversity of a cohort, scaffolding the emergence of collective imaginations. The ability to collectively reflect on the products of collective imagination—either in, or after, action—creates unity within diversity, forging a community of practice that actualizes what is imagined. Examples of these kinds of collaborative action-learning-imagining-reflecting-iterating practices are all around us in the folks that play or design massively multiplayer games, that play competitive sports, play in orchestras, orchestrate the production of movies, and so on.

The tools that today's students have to capture their own action and creative work, and to create platforms and practices for both individual and collective reflection, are immense. Furthermore, when they find that they need more knowledge or skills relative to their own domains, or suspect that there might be value in compelling adjacencies, they can seek these out almost effortlessly. Accessing and then putting new knowledge and skills into action as a community of practice supports a collaborative spiral learning. In many ways todays networked tools afford us unprecedented opportunities to honor the fundamentals of situated learning and cognitive apprenticeship that John Dewey laid out decades ago, but now with a breadth and depth, and at a scale of distributed participation that was unimaginable before.

In the genetic code of these new learning models, in what drives them, we find a certain promise...we see the possibility for...a kind of learning that builds capacity for agency in a uniquely disruptive time. And it does so honoring diversity. As a collaborative form of learning that honors diversity, individuals can participate from authentic perspectives.

Coming from this perspective I was excited to encounter Duhring and Snyder's new book—*New School, Old School.* At first I wondered...was this just a clever title or had they really stepped back and really thought through what might be a coherent new model of 21st Century education that honors the ways students, today, do learn and want to learn and that prepares them to be constant learners, creators, critical thinkers and productive mentors of each other. Their book provides fresh new ideas for constructing 'new school'—ideas that can be put into practice and, in fact, are being put into practice in places where few of us would expect to find cutting edge new ideas. One example: a school that focuses on learning for a cohort of highly diverse technical, design and artistically inclined kids. With today's tool set, embedded in a networked culture, amazing learning can happen in places where imaginations play an increasingly important role. Other examples abound. I hope you find their new book as provocative as I did.

QR codes are included in this book to help readers link to videos using their smartphones. This one is John Seely Brown on Motivating Learners (Big Thinkers Series) and can also be found at https://www.youtube.com/watch?v=41pNX9-yNu4

Our Proposition

It is easy to underestimate just how much students themselves adapt and grow while in college. Without question, much of their growth happens outside of the classroom and beyond the scope of most educational technologies. However, technology plays a central role in their learning. Today's classroom is not their only learning environment: they inhabit many different spaces outside the classroom and they have a spectrum of news feeds, social media and educational resources available to them at any moment, and in any location. Moreover, they are inspired by mentors, influenced by peers and required to respond to family, financial and health issues. They often juggle the problems they solve in class with the real world problem-solving they apply across a wide range of relationships while attending college. After all, they are transitioning from personal lives, surrounded by friends and family, to professional lives in which they interact with peers to make their way forward. Observing, measuring and guiding how they tap into the array of resources at their fingertips in order to explore, adapt and grow may well help to identify the most effective educational technologies.

DEBORAH SNYDER & JOHN DUHRING

Team Structures-Case Studies

When interviewing high performing college students on video, we have been struck by the mindsets at play and by the influence of peers and non-academic professionals on student learning. In particular, the team orientation students exhibit came as a surprise. In dozens of videos, a given student's identity and voice were influenced by their role in a team context as much as by the subject matter or an individual authority figure. By joining teams and taking on roles within team structures, their perspectives become more fluid than when working in isolation. They challenged themselves to explore what they offered the team as well as what they might take away as learning. In the words of one student, a "curriculum designed in which students do what they came to learn" might be the most effective environment for personal growth and professional development.

As an example, over the past three years, Cogswell College[1] students identified by faculty for their outstanding accomplishments in a class were interviewed on video. These students were first asked to describe what brought them to college. Their answers were typically either to follow a passion or because they felt a certain level of "fit" with the school's culture. They were then asked what they were working on at the time, and their answers skewed to highly technical deep dives into their roles on teams and what they were able to accomplish together. Finally, they were asked to reflect on what changed for them along the way. This consistent line of questioning enabled a surfacing of both external, team and academic factors.

---

1 Cogswell College was formed in 1887. http://www.cogswell.edu

4

The student videos represent student perspectives. As professionals, online portfolios provided through LinkedIn and other platforms offer a concise way to track paths after graduation. The qualities these students exhibit in order to make meaning out of their role in a team setting—becoming comfortable with ambiguity and the unknown, navigating by feedback, embracing a project bigger than oneself, imagining refinements along the way and diving into the flow of the process, even without a clear end point—might very well point to the future of higher education. Next are examples of students who engaged in personal explorations through teamwork and critically enhanced their college experiences.

A Software Engineer Learns by Tutoring Others

Aaron Cohn admitted he didn't apply himself at school until his schoolwork made a difference to others. He couldn't bring himself to commit to learning something simply to pass a test. He would even say he was lazy, doing just enough to get by. Yet, as a senior during his second try at college he developed a graphic user interface to a server farm that enabled students to manage the queue of jobs stacked up at the rendering engine at the end of every semester.

For this senior project, Aaron asked what he could build in service for the college, and the render farm bottleneck bubbled to the top. In order to build the system, he needed to teach himself a new language (Python), to understand the functions of the server and to recognize the needs of the non-technical students who used the system to render out their class and portfolio work at the end of each term. He said, "Now, you can control it. You can do your work if you need to without having somebody else's job start rendering while you are working. For them, this didn't exist before. They had a command-line tool. Artists do not do well with command lines!"[2]

He also put into play the listening and decoding skills he had developed as a tutor, mentoring other students who were in many cases like himself. Aaron mentioned right up front that he knew he was there to make a video of his front end app for the render farm but that he also wanted to talk about tutoring. When asked what he meant by tutoring, he revealed that he had discovered he learned best by tutoring other students. He found meaning by exploring how to reach the student he was tutoring. He actualized his potential when he actuated the potential of others. "I could see points where I wasn't reaching them, and I could see points where I was reaching them. It would be like a light switch, on or off. I was either really getting to them, or really not."

For Aaron, tutoring and mentoring others provided the structure and urgency he needed to commit himself fully. He recognized that through stepping up, by alerting others to the importance of what they were doing, he developed a professional voice. His willingness to commit himself as a tutor directly

---

2 Getting Creative with Software Engineering https://www.youtube.com/watch?v=M9X-ysSBNw_Y

influenced him to volunteer for the render farm project. The critical thinking skills he imparted to the students he mentored also helped him to identify the core problems students were having with the render farm and to design an appropriate solution.

"Critical thinking is a skill that you have to use in every aspect of your life. You cannot just take what you hear for granted. If you hear it, it doesn't necessarily mean it's true. Have the motivation to go on and verify it yourself. You have to be very careful because a lot of people have opinions and a lot of people have expertise where they want to come from their position of authority and tell you 'this is how it's done'. But, they are not necessarily telling you that. They are actually saying, 'this is the way I do it' and their perception is that's how it is done. So, look at a lot of different sources. Take what you can from your teachers, books, the Internet, wherever you can get all of your information. You combine all of those, and then you decide what the truth is."[3]

Aaron was hired as a Senior Associate Software Application Engineer at Workday, a company that was founded in 2005, went public in 2012, and now has over a billion dollars in yearly

---

3 Aaron Cohn Tutoring https://www.youtube.com/watch?v=wKd922oDtUU&t=4s

revenue. Workday provides SaaS-based enterprise solutions for their customer's human resources and financial management activities. While Aaron puts his technical knowledge to use in his career, the pathfinding methods he developed in college—including what serves to engage him fully by engaging others—have prepared him to operate in the most competitive and rewarding corporate settings.

A High School Physics Teacher Goes Full Stack By Getting Out of Town

Bakari Holmes was applying his degree in physics by teaching in high school when a representative from a college came to speak to his class about the benefits of hands-on, team-oriented learning made possible by working on real-world problems. In particular, the rep spoke about a video game program in which students designed and built apps in classes that are organized like studios and employ industry roles, methods and tools. Bakari had always loved video games and imagined how great it would be to participate in one of the most dynamic industries on earth.

As a new father, Bakari loved physics and enjoyed teaching, but had come to the realization that another career path might better enable him to provide for his family. For him, going back to college for another degree required a cost-benefit evaluation which would continually surface and guide his path going forward. Over the three years it took to get his new degree, Bakari would continually re-evaluate his position on his path towards this goal. The hands-on nature of his classes reinforced his decision. As his skill set evolved, so did his outlook on what was possible.

At first, Bakari thought his interest in music translated directly into designing the audio elements of games. He had always loved exploring musically, even publishing a Bobby McFerrin-style vocal solo on his zeemee.com portfolio.[4] He was inspired to explore how sound influences the behavior of players in video games just as they influence the emotional response of movie audiences. Exploring the world of sound design opened his eyes as well as his ears.

Bakari soon discovered that mobile games must use audio resources efficiently in order to respond to user behavior and to embrace a wide spectrum of sound designs. For instance, a sound like an explosion must be assembled algorithmically. By combining a "bing", a "bang" and a "boom" in different ways, a smart game developer can bring a wide variety of soundscapes to their work. When viewed from his cost-benefit perspective, Bakari saw his path veer towards hands-on programming. He wouldn't just produce the sounds, he would explore developing the games themselves.

For the summer before his senior year, Bakari landed an internship at the Sony Playstation program in San Diego, which led to a six-month consulting job at Sony Playstation in San Mateo. It was clear how important teamwork was for him in landing the consulting opportunity after his internship. "A lot of the people skills and passion that I have was really huge and stood out. Being able to answer questions about my previous experience, about what I did on teams, being specific about how that connects to being a successful candidate, that all stood out."[5]

---

4 Bakari Holmes on zeemee.com https://www.zeemee.com/bakariholmes
5 Bakari Holmes - Project-Based Classes and Working at Sony https://www.youtube.com/watch?v=d5JWh1y1fBE

After his experience working in San Diego and San Mateo, along with attending industry conferences and mixing with professionals in the field, Bakari's academic decisions now factored in not only his family interests but also honed in on the skills that would serve him best going forward. He became keenly aware of the wide range of technologies involved in delivering video games to users who ran them on mobile devices connected to the game and to others by networks. While he had already directed himself towards a career in the game industry, Bakari also saw the value brought about by a broadened perspective. In his final year of college, he set about to finish the courses needed to be a full-stack developer. He focused on the JavaScript/MEAN stack—including NodeJS, AngularJS, ExpressJS, MongoDB, ReactJS, and D3JS. As a generalist, he could address issues across an entire spectrum of connected devices, databases, networked APIs, and business logic to develop robust user experiences.

Bakari graduated with his second college degree in Software Engineering and was hired as a JavaScript Sr. Software Engineer with Accenture's Liquid Application Studio. His online portfolios not only feature him singing with his acapella group

"Business Casual", they highlight his fluency in interface design and passion for physics.[6]

Discovering the Future by Inventing Today

This book is informed by the personal transformations described by such students, with an eye towards improving higher education as it is more generally experienced. One theme emerges: in the practice of higher education, successful students repeatedly invent themselves. Regardless of what is assigned in class, they create roles for themselves to play with their peers. And, they discover new possibilities along the way. How they evolve as people goes hand in hand with their learning. Further examples:

One student started college in nursing to please her family, but then convinced them to support her to follow her dream of illustrating children's books by enrolling in an animation program. While working in team settings, she learned the value of storyboards, of documenting a story one scene at a time, one shot at a time, one static image at a time. This led her to pursue UX design, of developing digital user interfaces for desktop and hand held devices for commercial clients. After graduation, she mixed these skills when she designed "walk through" scenarios for the development team in a startup. Since she could tell the story of various types of potential customers in a wide variety of scenarios, she was asked to work with senior management to develop the story being told by the company to investors. After successfully raising funds based on the scenarios and stories they produced, she took on a new role, leading Public Relations.

6 http://bakariholmes.com/

Another student initially wanted to become an engineer, until a professor at his community college told him he probably would never use the formulas he was learning in class. He was told, "Computers do that now and in the future it will be even more so." Since what he liked most about engineering was drawing, he focused on that and transferred into a digital arts program. Through his involvement with the various clubs on campus, this student got involved in a short animation project and fell in love with the process of working with a small team. He said, "I didn't know it at the time, but I really liked 2D animation." He served as President of the Animation Club for two years and tutored drawing and animation students as well. After graduation, he was hired by a leading studio which specializes in 2D animations for film, TV and commercial clients.

Another student grew up with animated Disney films and always wanted to become an animator. When in college, she discovered something far more fundamental: she discovered the physics of motion and the anatomical elements that enable it. For a portfolio project, she rigged a 3D skeletal and muscular system for a rhinoceros that enabled the digital model to move realistically, flex its muscles and even blink its eyes. She also served as Lead Rigger and Technical Director for an award winning animated feature film produced entirely by students. She said, "Riggers have a little bit of say in how we tell the story, but for the most part we are the ones who are building the tools and building these rigs and sending them out into the world. We say, 'go, go make great things'. That is how we contribute to it." Along the way, she discovered that her attraction to the underlying structures that enable characters to come to life also applies to objects. By day, she now works at one of the world's premier animated film studios creating simulations of everything from clothing to seat belts, while at night she designs and fabricates custom bicycle frames and parts, which she offers to other enthusiasts.

There is also the mechanical engineering student who welds in her spare time, since she finds the process of welding and fabrication is a great way to reduce stress while validating some of her questions regarding the designs she develops. And there is the Game Design student who now applies the fundamentals of game mechanics, which he first put into practice while in college, to his role as a mid-level leader at one of the nation's most advanced children's hospitals. And there is the student who came to college after managing the acoustics and sound systems at his church, who then invented and developed a startup around an acoustic measuring device using Google's Tango sensors.

The cases provided by these outstanding students exemplify how widely variable and personal higher education outcomes can be. A course, in a given discipline, might actually serve to enable a student to explore and eventually excel in a completely unrelated area. We should become more aware of the multitude of personally meaningful and useful outcomes students discover as a result of their own explorations. These outcomes might well be the best measure of the success of their higher education experience. In particular, the adaptive mindsets that are developed in team settings deserve careful consideration and further research. The complex achievements and outcomes developed through such forms of open-ended exploration deserve greater recognition and appreciation.

Lessons from these Examples

S tudents going to college today learn as they go. They move freely using maps that never fail to bring them home. They make purchases without seeing a person and think nothing of it. They communicate with gestures, photos and sounds as well as words.

Why send these mobile, social and creative young adults to classrooms where they must listen to a single expert, to be graded on nothing related to their skills and passions? Why organize their education around the tools of an office when they live in a world of constant motion and change?

These same students will build autonomous vehicles and invent cities that revolve around people rather than cars. They will develop simulated worlds to augment the reality we experience today. They will employ transactional methods that remove accounting burdens and unlock prosperity. In colleges and universities today, we do them a disservice to ask them to check their imaginations at the door.

Fostering the ability to adapt to change and circumstance at a personal, group and societal level is perhaps the most important outcome of higher education. Think about it…why else do we spend so much time, effort, and money sending students through college?

And, if you consider the purposeful outcome of higher education is to create an environment where students are profoundly changed by their experience and learning, this book supports your view. Such is the goal of higher education. However, today there is much uncertainty regarding how to deliver on that goal.

As you observe higher education with fresh eyes you will begin to consider the structure of institutions in new ways, and appreciate how they must adapt to the challenges they now face. And, you will be asked to consider the possibilities of preparing students not only for the world that exists today but also for the ecosystems they will create in the future. In short, this book can be used to decode and re-think how we approach higher education and what is put into practice.

Higher Education Defined

The root word for "education" is to educe, or to "draw out." If we go back to the root meaning, ask yourself how we are going about this practice of "drawing out" students. Are there different ways to draw out learning? Apparently so. If that were not the case, we would not find ourselves in this ongoing debate of how best to educate our students.

Today's focus on curriculum and what needs to be learned and then assessed may be missing the boat. Delivery methods and teaching/learning styles may be missing the point. There is a bigger picture to focus on and that is how to draw learners out so that they can apply their learning beyond the classroom and take lessons that can be used to adapt as the environment continues to change. And it will change…that much we can be certain of.

There is unrest and frustration with the cost of education for the benefit many students and their families feel they receive. Too many college graduates and their families have discovered preparation for jobs and life after graduation lacking. Something has to give.

Too many students who attend college are walking away with little to show for their hard work. They might think the lectures they have attended and the papers they have researched and written have prepared them for life after college, but many college graduates are discovering they lack what it takes to join the teams spawned by dynamic economies. A recent survey by Inside Higher Ed found that while students think they understand foreign cultures, can apply critical thinking to complex problems or have the communications skills to work with people from different backgrounds, employers feel otherwise. [7]

With millions of employers looking for workplace talent and millions of college graduates looking for meaningful work, the current mismatch in higher education is painfully clear to parents and administrators as well as to recent graduates and hiring managers. In its "Education to Employment" series, the

---

[7] Well-Prepared in Their Own Eyes, https://www.insidehighered.com/news/2015/01/20/study-finds-big-gaps-between-student-and-employer-perceptions

McKinsey Center for Government suggested that education providers should work more closely with employers. [8]

Attempts at focusing on STEM (Science Technology, Engineering and Math) and with the addition of Art, STEAM, in order to better prepare students for jobs in high demand fields are moving in the right direction but this doesn't altogether remedy the mismatch of education and what society needs. Using new or reinvented learning methods like project-based learning, formative and adaptive feedback, learning outcomes assessments and other more measurable methods of instruction may or may not be effective depending upon the learning environment we create. It is not always about the technology we use to deliver the education. In fact, it is rarely about the technology but rather the opportunities we provide students to learn, whether it is technology enhanced or traditional classroom presentations and demonstrations.

The key here is that we owe it to students to help them reach their potential, prepare for the world of work and adapt to the changing ecosystem regardless of the new practices or policies we enact. The focus must shift toward producing competent professionals and enabling desired career outcomes. It must extend beyond the student graduating and the employer hiring, to prepare students for leading fulfilling lives doing things that personally matter.

In recent years, multiple attempts to disrupt the undergraduate college experience have surfaced. Online course delivery via the Internet, both synchronous and asynchronous, have entered the mainstream and continue to evolve. In Delaware, for instance, programs enable students to pursue advanced

---

8 Work Ready or Not, https://www.insidehighered.com/views/2014/04/04/address-ing-mismatch-between-colleges-and-job-market-essay

degrees while they also gain valuable real-world experience working full-time. [9]

Massive Open Online Courses, or MOOCs, caught the attention of the world when Dr. Sebastian Thrun of Stanford University launched his free course on Artificial Intelligence to Internet users around the world. More than 160,000 people signed up to take that course and other companies joined the rush to build free MOOCs.

Khan Academy created an international following when Salmon Kahn founded the free online tutorial site in 2006 mainly for math related topics. Today Khan Academy has over 2,400 video lessons online and they are still free. There is now a private Khan Lab School for students up to age 14 with a high school that launched in 2017. These are brick and mortar schools "dedicated to research-based instruction and furthering innovation" in education.

Udacity, an online technology training company founded by Dr. Sebastian Thrun, offers low cost nanodegrees designed to teach specific skillsets that employers want and need. The short, online courses are created to close the gap between higher education and the hiring workplace with skillsets that can be learned online and competency demonstrated through testing. It is still in the infancy stages of collaboration between the educator and the employers but nevertheless, companies like Udacity are finding and closing a gap that seeks to prepare people for jobs through a different form of higher education.

Many online learning pioneers outside of the higher education mainstream have focused their efforts on continuing

---

9 Online learning a mainstream option for Delaware higher education, http://www.delawarebusinesstimes.com/online-learning-a-mainstream-option-for-delaware-higher-education/

education and job training for employers, which happens to be a very big space. Non-accredited boot camps, badge systems and "unbundled learning" experiences are growing in popularity with their focus on preparing college graduates for jobs. Technology training organizations like General Assembly [10] are demonstrating that hands-on, team oriented experiences help experienced students embark on desirable careers. These pioneers challenge the very existence of traditional education and accreditation.

These alternatives are attempting to close the skills gap, but colleges must do more than train students for the world as we know it now. Preparing students for the world they are about to enter has always been the purpose of institutions of higher education. Tomorrow's great problems of traffic congestion, energy consumption and global economic interdependence cannot be addressed with simple "bootcamp" approaches. There is a place for higher education through colleges that embrace hands-on, team-oriented, real-world experiences.

In his 2015 commencement address to the graduates of Arizona State University (which boasts the largest student body in the United States), John Seely Brown [11] spoke of how the world we live in is unlike anything before. On the one hand, students must prepare for a world of increasing rates of change. On the other, they have tools at their disposal that enable them to make a difference and participate in that change. He likened their careers to a white water kayaker who must navigate each momentary turn, current, wave and eddy. Institutions of higher education and students have an opportunity here.

---

10 https://generalassemb.ly/
11 John Seely Brown was the Chief Scientist at Xerox, http://www.johnseelybrown.com/

In the following chapters we suggest strategies and methods that college administrators, faculty and staff can use to provide a college experience designed to prepare students for the ever-changing world in which they will work and live. These strategies go beyond subject matter learning and expertise to embrace the skills and industriousness needed to adapt to situations today's graduates will increasingly face, just like the kayaker mentioned by Dr. Brown at ASU.

Technologists can use this book as a starting point for building tools and services that truly add value to the process of higher education. Students have supercomputers in their pockets. They can re-orient themselves and coordinate their activities to take advantage of opportunities as they unfold. These tools bring radically new methods to gain perspective to both enrich and validate experience globally. By embracing each student's success, a special class of "new school" colleges are emerging as they unlock prosperity that was once only available to the wealthiest families and the highest achievers.

What Makes Higher Education Worthwhile?

Colleges are more than brands. They are cultural institutions. Colleges that have little or no brand recognition are doing extraordinary things. For instance, in its ranking for the top US colleges for international students, Forbes ranked Babson, Bryn Mawr, Claremont McKenna College, Mount Holyoke and Brandeis in their top 10.[12] Even colleges with little or no brand recognition are offering a unique experience in higher education that prepares students for the world they are about to enter.

Although there are over six thousand college campuses across the United States and several now offering degrees

12 50 Best U.S. Colleges For International Students 2016, http://www.forbes. com/sites/carolinehoward/2016/09/28/50-best-u-s-colleges-for-interna- tional-students-2016/#629f96bd1c8e

completely via the Internet, most people only think of the top 50 colleges as representing the whole. This is understandable since institutions of higher learning offer the same kinds of courses, give the same kinds of tests and offer the same kinds of degrees. Take a look at college websites to get a sense of how similar they have become. Look at their catalog and course offerings. Many catalogs look like the table of contents of a standardized textbook. Same, same, same.

Without a doubt, the experience at all colleges is not the same. While high quality may not be established by brand name, top company hiring managers don't often recruit at or offer the same jobs to graduates of all colleges. They want the best graduates so they go to the "best" colleges...the brand names we are familiar with. Venture capitalists don't fund business startup ideas from entrepreneurs across the board, either. They listen first to graduates, faculty, and students from the elite institutions. Why? Elite brand is assumed to equal higher quality. This is not true and it's not fair.

Alumni from elite institutions seek graduates from their own institutions. A Harvard or Stanford graduate, for instance, has been part of a culture that encourages networking. The selectivity exercised by elite colleges enables them to bring together students who have been the "best" in the communities they grew up in. Outside of class, they come together in study groups and social events alike. These graduates have an edge but it is not necessarily a reflection of what they are learning or how they will perform on the job.

As more colleges encourage team-based practices, classmates become colleagues and more alumni from less well-known schools will become more effective at supporting each other and pooling their resources. This bonding, the process of gaining perspective and of working through problems with peers is a benefit of attending an elite institution, but there are more. The elite college experience has the reputation that they prepare graduates to operate in the world around them. This is simply not sufficient in the white water world we live in today. Take a closer look at the lesser known schools. Don't count them out!

What's Different Today?

The college experience sets in place a world view and habits that will repeat themselves throughout careers and lives. Technology has widened the range of interactions possible. Social media has opened up opportunities to students, faculty, and alumni to network and communicate across geographic boundaries and share contacts, information, and collaborate on projects. No longer do a privileged few know the power of their networks and how to use them effectively. Students can work on projects with their friends and classmates even without going to class. For students with access to virtually all knowledge through the smartphones in their pockets, an elite college experience is being redefined.

Students today have the resources at their disposal to access knowledge and gain new perspectives. They can research any topic they wish from their home computers. Everyone who seeks to know something about a topic can "Google it".

Today, any college campus can become a place of privilege if used appropriately. Only in college will students mix so freely with others from a wide range of communities, skills and interests. They are surrounded by peers, mentors and experts who are available if they only take a moment to look for them. Taking advantage of the opportunities afforded by the college experience, faculty and staff can cultivate the passions and skills of their student body.

It has become obvious to some administrators, faculty, and parents that students can associate themselves with individuals and/or teams consisting of professional mentors as well as other students across a spectrum of fields of learning. They can meet virtually from almost anywhere in the world. Students can learn on their own and with expert guidance to design and run their own experiments. They have access to the right tools to build their own products and equipment. These and other opportunities once reserved to those in elite institutions have been democratized at a fundamental level. By providing scaffolding and guidance, colleges of all kinds can develop student talents that prepare them for professional success.

What makes a college experience valuable, then, is not the name of the institution but the purposefulness students apply to their own adaptations. Those who make the most of their environment, at any college, who learn to adapt with their classmates, who make things happen while they are in college, attract the attention of their peers, faculty, hiring managers and venture capitalists based on their skills and demonstrated performance. These students can create the careers they desire.

Higher Education: A Process, Not A Place

I t's something of a shock to many that overall college graduation rates in the United States hover around 60%. This
means almost half of all students drop out within 6 years
and most of them do not finish their degree.[13] Less than 33% of
Americans have attained at least a Bachelor's degree.[14] Finding
the college environment in which students will thrive, learn
and achieve success involves more than heritage, rankings and
reputation.

Students are encouraged to "find the right fit" when it
comes to choosing a college, and indeed the right place might

13 Graduation Rates: Six-Year Graduation Rates of Bachelor's Students - 2009, http://
www.higheredinfo.org/dbrowser/? level=nation&mode=map&state=0&submeasure=27
14 Graph: U.S. College Graduation Rates Are Rising, But the Rest of the World Is Catching Up, https://tcf.org/content/commentary/graph-u-s-college-graduation-rates-are-ris-
ing-but-the-rest-of-the-world-is-catching-up/

make all the difference. If a student is recruited for a specific project, or joins a club or team in their first semester or early in their career, this association might become the lifeline that propels them forward. Peers and play form the basis of identity and change, possibly as much as instruction.

Students should be encouraged to go where their curiosity will be awakened and where they can experience change first-hand rather than to the "best" school they can get into. This goes against the present tide, however, as more and more college bound seniors are counseled to reach for a short list of highly-regarded schools. Increasingly, students are hiring consultants to get into these elite" institutions. Getting accepted at a "safety" school may be considered a failure by the student and her family. And attend a school without a brand name or reputation? Unthinkable except for those who have few choices.

In addition to low graduation rates, increasingly, colleges are looking more deeply at high rates of attrition. In particular, US News reports that 1 in 3 first year students drop out.[15] They cite non-academic issues like family priorities, loneliness and financial constraints impacting the college experience for many students. With an average student lifetime of just over two years in many colleges, the efforts to keep students in college warrants major efforts in school spirit, housing and food services, along with tutoring, mentoring and counseling assistance.

Students want to do things, make things and be known for things. To illustrate this clearly, consider that all major state institutions and many smaller private colleges finance dozens of athletic teams knowing they can attract students who want

---

15 Freshman Retention Rate, http://colleges.usnews.rankingsandreviews.com/best-colleges/rankings/regional-colleges-west/freshmen-least-most-likely-return

to play their sport in college but would not make the team at an elite school. What else can we offer students that will do as much or more to prepare them for the world they will work in? There is an alternative.

New Tools for New Schools

New School tools make adaptation possible on a scale unimaginable before. College is a time to harness imagination through skill development. Today's students need to work with their hands as well as their minds. They need to move. They need to do things. Gone are the days that using your hands meant manual labor. So are the days when thinking was more valuable than making something happen. Now students communicate with instruments in their hands, through gestures. Working a smartphone is indeed the most sophisticated sign language ever created. Hands-on learning has entered an exciting, new phase that encourages imagination and innovation.

Smartphones, for example, provide the first wearable technology virtually all students bring with them to class. They walk along hallways focused on the screens they carry with them. They use a language of simple gestures to execute a complexity of tasks. A simple finger tap on the screen might snap a photo, send a message or execute a purchase.

These intelligent systems can either be used passively, replacing TVs, radios and telephones, or they can become powerful enablers for industrious, inquisitive imaginations. The cameras, maps and payment systems deployed through today's smartphones have already disrupted industries like ride-sharing, short-term lodging and vacation travel. Students entering college today are already skilled at the basics of what these and other technologies have to offer. What they lack is the deeper understanding and skills they need to take advantage of them as tools or to extend them in new ways. This can and should be the role of higher education.

Specifically, college students should learn to appreciate the world around them by using the tools in their own pockets and hands, with faculty guidance. They can explore questions, so they should be asked to discover news and current research with specific implications on class assignments. They can explore maps at any time, and they should use them to understand the dynamics, history and geometry unfolding around them, even by playing a game like Ingress, Pokemon Go or through rapidly evolving augmented realities. They can code up new worlds, providing them with the challenge of applying physics that mimic our own or choosing to invent their own rules. They can literally rewrite textbooks together. The entire college curriculum, from humanities through sciences, is being transformed by how students augment their intelligence through the technology they now have at their disposal.

College courses should be learning laboratories, so students build their capabilities using and applying technologies to deepen their understanding. A graduate-education model that puts projects at the core of the student experience inspires students to deep dive into subject matter within the context of the projects they work on.

The New Age of Inquiry

Something magical happens when students are encouraged to take control of their learning journey. As they develop their observational skills, questions form regularly from their experience. They search naturally and immediately using whatever technology and resources are at their disposal. They seek out points of view as they make sense of the feedback they have assembled through their research. They deal with authority and meaning developed from fresh data. With a digital device or smartphone, any student becomes an "expert" in record time. But, how can they prepare themselves to act on what they have learned?

Traditional college curriculum has become limited in offering opportunities for student-led inquiry. The assumed "rightness" of knowledge being delivered gets in the way, regardless of how esteemed the source. Some very bright students have quit college and gone on to do great things (think Steve Jobs and Mark Zuckerberg) when they discovered their own methods were more effective for them. There seems to be acceptance that "wisdom" sits at the top of the hierarchy of knowledge.[16]

Passing on knowledge, from professor to student, is old school. Today's changing world needs college graduates who can figure things out and do things with what they have learned, on their own or with their colleagues. Change will continue as a fact of life. How they observe, process and adapt is the value of their higher education.

The Importance of Inquiry

This perspective builds on an "old school" approach to higher education promoted by John Dewey in the early 1900s. As noted in his biography by the Internet Encyclopedia of Philosophy, Dewey maintained that "Inquiry should not be understood as

---

16 Knowledge Hierarchy, https://www.flickr.com/photos/yyq123/70744379

consisting of a mind passively observing the world and drawing from this ideas that if true correspond to reality."[17] Rather, it is as an active process which includes active manipulation of the environment to test hypotheses, and results in adaptation to the environment.

In other words, learning is the byproduct of adaptation, not the goal unto itself. Skills are important and to be mastered such that by graduation, students fluidly apply the critical thinking and decision making that comes from their use. By developing communications, critical thinking and decision making skills augmented by technologies that reach around the world, the college experience should generate a sense of industriousness and agency to match students' conceptual awareness. Through the skills they acquire, they can literally see the world in new ways.

---

17 John Dewey (1859—1952), http://www.iep.utm.edu/dewey/

Old School

Historically, the growth of schools has been punctuated by societies adapting to changing circumstances. Now colleges, once only training grounds for religious and political leaders, play a pivotal role in preparing students to adapt to new ways of life and act as gateways to modern economies and personal prosperity. Encyclopedia Britannica reports that the people in North America, Europe and Oceania send over 60% of their 18-24 year old populations to college.[18] At the same time, Brazil, China, India, Nigeria, Cuba and South Korea have seen large recent growth in the percentage of their populations going to college as their economies have become increasingly interdependent.

---

18 The development and growth of national education systems, https://www.britannica. com/topic/education/Global-trends-in-education

Schools and colleges afforded students the opportunity to grow in a new and better way. For example, as industrialism spread in Great Britain in the 1800s, writer Charles Dickens described the horrors of children working in factories. The cultural response was to outlaw many employment practices. This led to the need to provide other activities for children and schools grew to accept an increased population of students. Until that time, major systems of education prior to college did not formally exist.

In the United States, rising industrialism in the early 1900s affected 90% of the population who used to work on family farms. When mechanical tractors dramatically reduced the labor required in farm operations, communities could see their way of life was going to change. High schools were created to help the transition from farm life to city life. This transition accelerated at the end of World War II, which brought with it the GI Bill (called the Servicemen's Readjustment Act of 1944) to cause an explosion of interest in colleges and universities.

The tremendous growth of college students brought by both the GI Bill and the following baby boom accompanied a time of prosperity and a need for professional workers. For many, college was a time to see the world in a new way, to embrace new ideas and to think through problems systematically. A "well-rounded" student could graduate into professional schools or corporate training programs once they entered the work force. A trickle-down effect took place after college. As more college graduates became trainees, then managers and leaders, more entry level professional jobs required a college degree.

As the economy was increasingly supplied by a college-educated workforce, colleges also looked within themselves to find and train faculty and resources needed for their own growth.

Here, academia had a distinct advantage. The best students could be identified while in college and often encouraged to continue their studies to pursue promising academic careers.

With the best and brightest often guided to pursue academic research and achieving tenured professorial roles, curricula in many fields blossomed to reflect their pursuits, creating new specialties. Along the way, an industry of publishers made it possible for graduates to fine-tune their academic interests, to identify leaders in their fields of study, and to develop and promote their own careers through research and publications.

However, while scholarly publications continued to support the development of new fields of study, many introductory level courses became standardized. Publishers discovered that political science topics taught at the University of Michigan could be easily replicated at other colleges, which meant more sales of introductory textbooks even if those books didn't exactly replicate a University of Michigan experience. In most college environments, this encouraged professors to measure students against standard expectations using objectives, assignments and tests generated by commercial publishers.

According to the Babson Survey Research Group, some twenty million students attend college each year.[19] So, a textbook written by a famous professor at an elite institution potentially attracted sales across a vast landscape of colleges. With the goal of disseminating a body of knowledge to their students, instructors who determined which books to require for their courses more often than not chose a textbook reputed as the top in the field. Specialized or local topics, as a consequence, faded from introductory courses which became increasingly driven by standardized textbook content.

---

19 Download their report, "Grade Increase", at http://www.onlinelearningsurvey.com/

Without question, this shift had a profound impact on how and what students experienced in college. Textbooks were the same, curriculum similar, and assessment methods standardized. Many parents and prospective students, assume that the experience and education a student receives at the college they choose reflects that college's reputation and brand. Stronger brand name, better education. Weaker brand name, perhaps not as good an education. No brand name, poor quality education. This is not necessarily the case.

Long gone are the days of farm children growing up and studying in one room school houses, the norm in the late 1800s. Taken in context of industrialization, rural families sought to prepare their children for life beyond the farm, which in those days meant "behind a desk". The best students would become managers, processing forms and directives. The less academically inclined students would work with their hands.

In the days of the one room schoolhouse, all ages and skill levels sat together behind desks in rows designed to simulate the state-of-the-art manufacturing working environments they could now aspire to. They were taught manners, how to behave for the new world that was taking shape. They were introduced to reading books that conveyed information and inspired bright minds.

In those days, there was plenty of free time to play, to pursue interests outside of lessons. Students could associate with each other as they saw fit. They gained their identity within the school, along with their peers. Their goal was not to go to college. The purpose of their education was to be equipped to find employment and pursue interests outside of the school environment.

The one-room school example illustrates a primary pre-requisite for education to take place: seeing the world directly. As with John Seely Brown's metaphor of white water kayaking, on an individual level, adaptation requires direct observation and a new point of view.

Unfortunately today, discovery and time to play has not been the focus in many school systems due to the focus on the three Rs and standardized testing to measure learning. What was once called "show and tell", where students are encouraged to share things and take turns telling stories about their experiences outside of class, takes so much time away from other activities, the practice hardly exists anymore except in the most basic level of classwork. Without such direct and public feedback that this form of learning offers from peers at school, students increasingly measure themselves by the tests, grades and merit badges doled out by authority figures, typically their teachers. The resulting loss of personal identity is one unintended consequence of so much formal structure and oversight without the free play needed to support natural adaptation.

This lack of perspective in not limited to the United States. As more international students fill classrooms, colleges find that many countries rely even more heavily on testing in their school systems. With fewer extra-curricular opportunities to develop real-world observational skills and feedback, many students approach higher education as more of the same.

American Scholar to Global Player

In 1837, the eminent American writer Ralph Waldo Emerson delivered an address to the Phi Beta Kappa society at Harvard which has set the tone for higher education ever since. Phi Beta Kappa is America's oldest and most widely recognized collegiate honor society and a leading advocate for the liberal arts and sciences at the undergraduate level.

Emerson's essay spoke of the American Scholar. The resonance of his vision continues strongly to this day and should be understood deeply whenever we talk about higher education. His presentation is readily accessible.[20]

Emerson spoke at a time when industrialization was in it's infancy. Steam-powered locomotion was catching on and Morse sent his first coded electrical telegram a year later. These two technologies provided the foundation for what lay just ahead, empowering far-sighted entrepreneurs to build empires rivaling those of any government.

Emerson must have sensed the cultural shifts that would come, in which any man could live by his wits and his industriousness. We live now at a similar time of radical change, in which transformative technologies are available to a much wider population around the globe. The guidance Emerson gave to his audience of the "best and brightest" at Harvard now applies to every student entering in higher education.

Decoding his messages into today's language can provide something of a Rosetta Stone to understand what higher education should be and how it will continue to grow and prosper given the right strategy and direction. It's remarkable how what he has to say reflects what has been said throughout history. Not a new message, but one that stands the test of time and one that we must apply today in order to be perceived to add value and be around tomorrow.

---

20 The American Scholar, http://www.emersoncentral.com/amscholar.htm

Emerson distinguished higher education in no uncertain terms. He speaks of a highly specialized society, in which the planter never interacts with the gatherer on the farm. Each becomes diminished to the level of their trade and not "Man on the farm." He applies this perspective to include the trades-man (who "scarcely ever gives an ideal worth to his work, but is ridden by the routine of his craft, and the soul is subject to dollars"), the priest, the attorney, the mechanic and the sailor.

He then speaks to how each of these can regain their full selves ("the right state") and to reap the rewards of "Man Thinking." Importantly, he distinguishes this condition from merely thinking, "or still worse, the parrot of other men's thinking."

While he had no words for imagination, curiosity, or creativity, it is striking how powerfully his message would address what is lacking in what we now call higher education. This speech has been famously referred to as an "Intellectual Declaration of Independence."[21] Unfortunately, what Emerson suggested was re-imagined again in 1893, as the need for factory workers prompted an assembly-line approach to education which has persisted to this day.[22]

The process of preparing students for tests rather than life itself was born then and has produced many students without a solid sense of purpose or direction. Much of secondary schooling today is by the book and by the bell, without much room for play, imagination or invention. This leads to a lack of resiliency, the disposition formed by the process of exploring

---

21 Intellectual Declaration of Independence, http://laurenolson.blogspot.com/2008/11/intellectual-declaration-of.html

22 A venture capitalist searches for the purpose of school. Here's what he found, https://www.washingtonpost.com/news/answer-sheet/wp/2015/11/03/a-venture-capitalist-searches-for-the-purpose-of-school-heres-what-he-found/?utm_term=.9688199f5a00

problems that they don't know how to solve initially. Because they haven't experienced how to do this, students who continue to pass through the motions of old school study without experiencing what higher education should be risk being lost, unprepared for a world of change without the tools to work in a changing landscape full of problems waiting for solution and opportunities waiting for discovery.

Higher education at an individual level consists of imagination and scientific reasoning coupled with action to facilitate personal growth. Whether the description comes from Plato, Leonardo da Vinci, Ralph Waldo Emerson, or John Seely Brown, what they argue hasn't changed much over centuries of human adaptation.

At certain points within people's lives, they have a choice to change in a fundamental way. This is not "schooling", in which someone tells them what to do and then measures their progress. This is their choice to play with something new, to examine what is in front of them and to act with conviction even when the answer is not certain. To make mistakes along the way brings them closer to understanding.

Clock and Seat Time

"Old school" boundaries are governed by the clock and "seat time", which lose their meaning in "new school" thinking. "New school" students today working on an illustrated e-book, a video game, an animation or film fall into time warps in which hours seem to fly by. They imagine ways to animate what they are doing, to inject temporal elements into their work, to elaborate on their compositions.

Their tools can be a word processor, a spreadsheet, a digital audio workstation (a DAW), an integrated development environment (IDE), an augmented or virtual reality platform or an animation workspace. Using these tools as part of a team to bring stories to life moves students into worlds they have never imagined before.

In the midst of creating a collaborative, large-scale composition, they dive into a flow state in which they execute their technique and their work meld into an alternative reality. They step aside from their ordinary reality and lose themselves in something that flows through them, something that shows them who they are in way far removed from what happens in a classroom.

As descried eloquently by Mihaly Csikszentmihalyi in his famous TED talk on flow, this state defines a kind of success.[23] Having flow while you are working has never been the goal of "old school" education. But, to be aware of a mission of improving society, of engaging students in meaningful work, experiencing flow is a desired state for all students. When the state of flow is engaged, the work is being done for its own sake.

As students engage in more challenging assignments, pushed beyond their comfort zone, they adapt by increasing their skill levels so as to contribute more effectively. They think more critically of their part of the overall project. They embark on their work as a mission.

Traditionally, students have been known to "burn the midnight oil" as they cram for tests, and in the process some of them discover this sense of alternative reality. Unfortunately, they often have nothing to show for their work beyond a grade,

23 Flow, the secret to happiness, https://www.ted.com/talks/mihaly_csikszentmihalyi_on_flow

the goal in the "Old School" environment.

"New School" students seek to create things of lasting value along with a feeling of contributing to the greater good. They use it as a moral barometer. They experience flow even through Instagram and video games. Why should they set it aside when they set foot on campus or sign into an online course or even when participating in a MOOC?

Developing ideas from the earliest sketch through to complex compositions that are available to the world goes far beyond what is called "project-based learning." It can be described as "projects on top of projects built by other projects", all of them organized by a production pipeline. A video game might have 10,000 files submitted to a version control system: some art, some sound, some code. A novel requires hundreds of thousands of edits and rewrites.

These are the kinds of projects that inspire students to go beyond their abilities. Through these projects, students can be measured not only by their achievements, but how they explain their roles and their contributions to the process. They should be able to also describe what challenged them and how they adapted through critical thinking and other outcomes.

In college, students can try out what they need to take into their careers, and to become successful in life. The new school approach creates an atmosphere where students compare and contrast their own approaches with peers and mentors as they learn. They are challenged to observe themselves and others in order to find their own identity, to imagine what comes next, to develop roles they can play in a variety of environments, and to organize themselves to operate in the world they will step into after graduation.

Experience Plus Knowledge

When it comes to reforming higher education, scholars and educational technology professionals alike extoll the value of the "guide on the side" as opposed to the "sage on the stage." Others debate the value of "skills" vs "knowledge." These arguments evaporate when considering what forces adaptation and learning at a behavioral level. Recent investigations of brain activity surface surprising evidence: learning is caused by systematic use of voluntary motion. The Christoper and Dana Reeves Foundations published:

"Neurons in the motor cortex, the region of the brain that controls voluntary movement, send their axons through the corticospinal tract to connect with motor neurons in the spinal cord. The spinal motor neurons project out of the cord to the correct muscles via the ventral root. These connections control conscious movements, such as writing and running."[24] The process of adaptation forces decisions that effect change. Physical movement, tied to kinesthetic sensing, creates new neural pathways.

In the same way, students are quite literally building new worlds as they engage in the process of adaptation that the environment of higher education provides. Limiting the scope of their construction efforts narrows their options. Without a doubt, new school colleges will adapt more effectively by considering the student experience first, more deeply now than ever before.

Draw Out Learning... Literally

It may seem ironic to go back to the earliest Greeks for a lesson but Plato pretty much nailed it. In one instance, he described for students a scenario in which prisoners were chained from birth facing a wall inside a cave, with their backs to the cave opening and to the outer world. They saw the world outside the cave only as shadows as they were projected on the wall by the light of the sun.

At some point, the chains of the prisoners melted away and one of them used his freedom to find the cave opening and step outside. At first he was blinded by the light, but then he eventually adapted. He saw that this was the real world and he learned to understand it and to find his way within it. Of course, when he went back into the cave to tell his friends they

---

24 What is the central nervous system? http://www.christopherreeve.org/site/c.ddJFKRN-oFiG/b.4452147/k.6085/Voluntary_and_Involuntary_Movement.htm

didn't believe nor did they wish to look at the world he described. [25]

Plato's parable of the cave describes the challenge of educating individuals and groups whose only life experiences are like flickering reflected images on a cave wall. Using modern terms, Plato might well be describing a mediated world not unlike what children today often see through the music, movies, video games and social media of modern culture. They are growing up in a culture that only connects them to the world through technology. Is this enough?

A recent news article provides a somewhat dramatic view from the chief executive of the UK's Independent Association of Prep Schools, who says that parents who shield their children from challenges and failure hinder their development even before they are college age:

He warns that overly sheltered children "are never going to cope in the real world. Many parents drive their children to school and the children never learn common sense rules of being a pedestrian. They are clueless about crossing the road."[26]

These children have been raised by a new breed, the "helicopter parent." To address their concerns, colleges are developing Parental Relations offices and increased focus on graduation and placement rates.[27] But these approaches attack the symptoms. They don't address the core problem. Even in a

---

25 Plato's Allegory of the Cave - Alex Gendler, https://www.youtube.com/watch?v=1R-WOpQXTltA
26 Anxious parents 'breed generation of clueless children', says schools leader, http://www.telegraph.co.uk/education/educationnews/11891626/Anxious-parents-breed-generation-of-clueless-children-says-schools-leader.html
27 Managing Millennial Parents, http://chronicle.com/article/Managing-Millennial-Parents/130146/

world where parents feel they need to be ultra vigilant in protecting their children, there must be an environment where students can learn how to adapt, learn common sense lessons, learn to operate in an ecosystem of change. The expense of doing otherwise is simply too high.

The "college experience" has been and will continue to be one of adaptation. By the time students begin college, they have developed their sense of the world around them through the lens provided by family and community life. "Going off to college" has become a cultural rite that entrusts children to take on the responsibilities of an adult in a seemingly safe learning environment. Our current system of colleges and universities has enabled the transformation from private life to professional life for millions of people.

However, for many families, the criteria they use for choosing a college might be out of touch with the goal of preparing their child for life after college. Does the football team really matter? A sorority? A lecture hall? Students yearn to apply their imaginations to meaningful activities, to develop their unique skill sets in order to make teams better, to make a difference by what they do. Colleges can do a better job providing hands-on experiences that harness students' imagination while at the same time revealing pathways to apply their skills as they go out into the world on their own.

Adaptation Can Happen Anywhere

Faculty and administrators need to foster such a "can-do" environment in every classroom, lab and lecture hall or risk losing their students and their own relevance. They can pull into every course and degree elements of design, art, engineering and management to foster collaborations that require students to listen carefully to each other and to others more generally. The privilege afforded students through this approach enables their sense of self, of agency in the world, to blossom.

College represents an opportunity in which to develop skills, knowledge and a questing disposition. From the moment students set foot on campus, they are afforded a unique set of relationships and opportunities regardless of the institution they attend, what books are assigned and the makeup of their classmates. Well-known "brand name" universities have developed the networks and methods for not only selecting the best students for their institution, but also encouraging them to effectively use the resources at their disposal.

As more colleges provide hands-on, team-oriented curricula that address real-world problems, their students will put into practice as professionals what has brought them success in college. In spite of a disparity in physical resources, all colleges have the potential to create an environment that encourages the personal transformations that occur and the cultures that they cultivate.

Measuring Adaptation

Colleges need to measure students as they move, as they adapt, and as they achieve. This is different from attempts to measure "learning" as an outcome. Learning outcomes, such as written and oral communications, critical and creative thinking, informational literacy and quantitative reasoning, can be measured by tests and assignments using "old school" methods. But, when a "new school" approach is taken, students learn the nuances of critique within team settings: to provide feedback to their peers and mentors as well as to accept face-to-face feedback themselves. These students carry with them not only an operating system based on their unique skill set and disposition, but also an ability to commit wholeheartedly to the task at hand.

This capacity to give full measure comes only through achievement and the development of successful habits. Higher education, particularly as instilled in college, is not about "passing through", but about measuring oneself in order to adapt and change.

A wonderful graduate course run by the author Ken Kesey in 1987 at the University of Oregon illustrates the value of applying real-world measures to college work, even thirty years ago. His creative writing course involved students who were mobile and measured as they collaborated on a large scale project which itself resulted in a commercially published book.

In this example, students are encouraged to play: both to let ideas take shape organically and to develop a sense of team dynamics. They then develop a skillset customized for the task at hand and sketch out the elements of each composition. The composition involves development of characters, their roles in scenarios, and the stories that surface through their behaviors.

Significantly, once a system of operations is in place, students must render out their contributions to the composition in a professional atmosphere. The result is an industrial-strength outcome from students while in college.[28]

In two semesters, Kesey's group of students would produce

---

28 Ken Kesey's Eclectic Writing Acid Test, http://www.rollingstone.com/culture/features/ken-keseys-eclectic-writing-acid-test-19891005

one of the first collaborative novels ever accepted for publication by an established commercial publishing house, Viking Press. The methods he developed with his students shed light not only what is possible in college, but instills the notion that Kesey's reasoning was sound when he announced he was discarding his literary career in order to "live a novel rather than to write one." His methods have been adapted, famously, in many professional endeavors. For instance, the Whole Earth Catalog reflects his way of tinkering, of scrabbling things together and living in new ways. This "new school" of thinking influenced young students like Steve Jobs and other technologists.

With just a bit of tweaking, this one creative writing course is an example of what can be replicated in colleges around the globe. It represents a meaningful assignment, a comprehensive challenge with measurable results. It was designed so each student could draw on the experience throughout their professional careers.

This passage from the *Rolling Stone* article reveals the "new school" thinking at the root of the course: "The idea of collaborating on a novel with a group of students first came to Kesey several years ago. He had been to a couple of university writing programs, doing the usual gig of a visiting author: leading workshops, reading student manuscripts and critiquing them. What he read disturbed him—not because the writing was raw, weird or unsettling, but because it wasn't.

"The stories were well crafted; all contained the requisite amounts of character development, dramatic conflict and resolution. But they were empty at the center, dead on the page. They were so carefully designed that they never came truly alive. The problem, Kesey concluded, lay not with the young writers themselves; there was plenty of talent chained beneath the forged-iron prose. The problem lay with the academic system that had produced them."

The goal was to create a novel in the course and to have it published. To do so, students would be exposed directly to the issues and time-frames required in a professional setting. He organized the course to mentor the students in something of a studio model. They would work together on a real manuscript, from concept to research, character development, plot and style. So, the course would depart from "old school" theoretical underpinnings. It would be messy. It would move the students into uncharted territory. They would have to adapt to complete their assignment within two semesters.

Unlike a traditional approach, Kesey set up his class to work as a group of professionals. He might as well have had them developing an app, a video game or an animated film, if it were present time. The class started with a goal and the students would have to use their wits to bring the project to completion. All the tools the students needed were readily available but the pipeline knowledge, the experience of working a project from concept to execution, was new. The metrics he set in place helped organize the group.

In this course, Kesey's students were exposed to what underpins the publishing process. Making a published book went far beyond "writing" as it is traditionally taught. They experienced the values associated with collaborating in the publishing process. Colleges today can devise production pipelines that result in media, apps, and intelligent devices. In these projects, which can last several semesters in which students must wrap up their work in order to be carried on by the next cohort, professional environments are effectively simulated.

Actualizing Through Adaptation

Applying technology across the spectrum of academia goes beyond using computers in classrooms. The possibilities to actively design and create offers students opportunities to develop their capacity to pursue professional careers. At Stanford, for instance, students are encouraged to take a least an introductory computer class. "Stanford is the intellectual heart of Silicon Valley. Stanford students quickly come to understand that they should take at least one of the introductory computer science courses, which are very much part of the culture," said Eric Roberts, computer science professor. Across the board, Stanford students are encouraged to get into tech as deeply as they can as undergraduates.[29]

Academically, the recent "Digital Humanities" movement embraces a wide range of methods and practices which promise to change how students explore, coordinate their work and publish their results. For example, practitioners in DH engage in manipulating large data sets, exploring 3D modeling of historical artifacts, publishing "born digital" dissertations, even fomenting hashtag activism.[30] It's being called "the most exciting field you've never heard of."[31] Simply put, it is humanities as practiced in 2017 and going forward. It draws on technologies to support inquiry, exploration and prototyping. Increasingly, these are the skills hiring managers are looking for.

---

29 Computer science becomes Stanford's most popular major, http://www.mercurynews.com/2012/07/27/computer-science-becomes-stanfords-most-popular-major/
30 Debates in the Digital Humanities http://dhdebates.gc.cuny.edu/debates?-data=toc-open
31 The Most Exciting Field You've Never Heard Of http://www.pcmag.com/commentary/350984/digital-humanities-the-most-exciting-field-youve-never-hea

With millions of tech-related jobs searching for talent, undergrads have ground-floor opportunities at their fingertips. At the same time, hiring managers express their frustration by how ill-prepared college students are. Says one, "I need people who can use GIT (Global Information Tracker), write coherently about how to build and run software, debug and patch with impunity, and spin up and optimize virtual servers on a variety of environments. Neither code schools nor computer science programs seem to produce talent like this. And there are few resources for teaching these kind of skills."[32]

Hiring managers report they go out of their way to dig into what makes students tick in order to determine if there is a good fit for the organization's needs. They want students who know how to function as part of a team, who can move between roles and adapt their skill set to the needs of the organization.[33] Ultimately, college graduates should be able to commit themselves to their pursuits, actualizing their passions and unique skills, just as a college athlete prepares for a professional career.

The New School college curriculum should be designed such that students do what they came to learn. Researchers like Don Tapscott say the age-old model of teaching doesn't work anymore. The publishing model, of transferring information from the lecturer to the student, just isn't enough in a world where students can instantly engage minds from all over the world in order to build something. Tapscott warns, "If campuses are seen as places where learning is inferior to

32 Please don't learn to code, learn to understand code instead, https://medium.com/@melissamcewen/please-dont-learn-to-code-learn-to-understand-code-instead-7bd-9895cfb92#.hijsrftd4
33 What hiring managers are really trying to figure out when they ask, 'What are your hobbies?' http://www.businessinsider.com/how-to-answer-hobbies-interview-question-2016-5?r=UK&IR=T

other models, or worse, places where learning is restricted and stifled, the role of the campus experience will be undermined as well. The university is too costly to be simply an extended summer camp."[34]

Tesla founder Elon Musk appears to agree when he says, "Forty years ago we had pong. Like, two rectangles and a dot. That was what games were. Now, 40 years later, we have photorealistic, 3D simulations with millions of people playing simultaneously, and it's getting better every year. If you assume any rate of improvement at all, then the games will soon become indistinguishable from reality."[35]

Over 300 colleges and universities have established degree-granting baccalaureate programs in Video Game Design. What if going to college was more like working in a game development studio? That is exactly what drives the curriculum at Cogswell College in San Jose, California.[36] Students earn a fully accredited bachelors degree while gaining valuable industry experience by working with real clients and their peers to produce real games. Somewhat surprisingly, the "soft skills" of creative storytelling, critical thinking and managing multi-disciplinary teams provides the essence of the professional they become along the way. The roles they play mirror the jobs found in industry, many of which didn't exist 10 years ago.

Entertainment Design Artist Katie Fortune now works at Machine Zone, makers of the popular Mobile Strike mobile

34 Universities must enter the digital age or risk facing irrelevance, https://www.thestar.com/news/canada/2016/05/10/universities-must-enter-the-digital-age-or-risk-facing-irrelevance.html
35 Elon Musk Thinks That Our Existence Is Someone Else's Video Game, http://www.huffingtonpost.com/entry/elon-musk-simulation-reality_us_57506989e4b0c3752dccceb2
36 Preparing Students for Professional Game-Design Careers, http://www.joanganzcooneycenter.org/2016/07/28/preparing-students-for-professional-careers/

game. In college she learned to adapt her visual art skills to storyboarding and working with engineers to build interactive experiences. The Glassdoor.com salary database reports starting salaries for 2D artists, with the ability to sketch out characters, scenarios and stories, average above $50,000 per year.[37]

Technical Artist Bugi Kaigwa works at Visual Concepts, the developer behind Take-Two's interactive sports games, such as NBA2K. Technical artists develop the "rigging" of digital characters, the handles and structures that enable animators to make them move realistically. Glassdoor sites beginning technical artists average salaries of over $60,000 per year. In college, he learned to manage teams of artists to integrate sound, motion and graphics into the overall video game design.

A game design engineering student worked at Google and then joined a start-up as co-founder. Typically, college students do not gain management experience while in college. Video game engineering managers salaries start over $65,000 per year, reports Glassdoor. By managing teams of students to integrate the functionality required on a game project, the student knew he was gaining valuable industry experience.[38]

Every video game injects realism into the experience through interactive sound design that maps to user behaviors. A digital audio production student works as a Senior Software Engineer at Disney Interactive. Glassdoor suggests that starting sound engineering salaries start around $60,000. By implementing interactive features such as modifying the volume associated with a character's movements while they are "invisible" in the game, this student leveraged both the artwork and audio assets

---

37 The Art of Teamwork, https://www.youtube.com/watch?v=BLNCMjhZhcc&feature=youtu.be
38 From Game Concept to Full Mobile Game - How Students Made "Tangram Jam" https://youtu.be/7NQR16wPsZI

developed by other students on his team.[39]

Working across talented teams takes special skills. A game design student works for Microsoft as a Game Evangelist. According to Glassdoor, developer relations salaries start at $60,000. This student found that the serendipity provided at Game Development Club meetings was enhanced simply by buying pizza and encouraging students to bounce ideas off of each other.[40]

While these examples stress salaries, it is the agency developed in a "new school" environment that has made these graduates so attractive. The value of a hands-on, team-based college experience is instantly recognizable to hiring managers. To them, growing their culture is what leads to success. For their part, Google says, "It's really the people that make Google the kind of company it is. We hire people who are smart and determined, and we favor ability over experience."[41] Organizations like Google actually favor recent graduates, which makes the changes taking place in higher education all the more important.

These examples illustrate the relationship between actualization and adaptation. The process of iterating, retooling and fine tuning leads to actualization and reveals an ability to adapt and apply to new situations as they arise. This is a critical element of success beyond college.

---

39 Programming the Sound for Video Game "Wizard's Prison", https://youtu.be/MQKk-GxHXLsM
40 Tobiah Marks, https://youtu.be/OZ8bnT1tEPg
41 Our culture, https://www.google.com/about/company/facts/culture/

What Do Emerging Ecosystems Need?

One innovation developed in the 1970s was the practice of venture capital. It differs from traditional banking in a fundamental way: it values potential as an asset. Currently, 43% of Fortune 500 companies founded since 1979 were funded through venture capital. These account for 57% of the total market value of all such companies. They also account for over 80% of all research and development spending. They employ over 4 million people.[42]

This means that colleges and universities, often the funnel for government research investments, may no longer manage the lion's share of funding or jobs in research. As an alternative, they should pay close attention to the companies that

---

42 How Much Does Venture Capital Drive the U.S. Economy? https://www.gsb.stanford.edu/insights/how-much-does-venture-capital-drive-us-economy

receive venture capital. It turns out, startups that have received venture funding love to work directly with students. Unlike governments, whose funding protocols involve grant-writing and stringent compliance guidelines, venture-capitalized companies tend to be nimble and value student perspective, since these represent their future customers.

To understand where venture capital flows is to gain a glimpse into the world of tomorrow. Mature venture-backed companies like Apple, Google, Microsoft, Amazon and Facebook gain the headlines, but alongside them are thousands of amazing ventures who are looking for feedback, for their new customers and for talent. Universities already provide user testing grounds, developer talent and feedback on prototypes as well and finished products. These companies pride themselves on learning fast as they grow.

Preparation in Practice

Preparing students to be a part of the ecosystems of tomorrow has to become the focus for every educational institution. The current structures will not hold up much longer using the "old school" approach.

The costs of higher education in many instances outweigh their benefits. Most students are saddled with sizable financial debt from student loans. From purely a financial standpoint, many students would be better off finding a job after high school. Those students can advance in their careers earlier and make money while those going to college are paying for over four years and may not be able to make up the difference considering they must pay back loans. A recent analysis published by Bloomberg noted:

"On average, college pays off, though not always. The wage premium comes with risk. For every degree short of a graduate degree, there's a decent chance that a good high school graduate will out-earn the college graduate."[43]

This mismatch cannot last, but there is still value in higher education, but only if done correctly. Teamwork, projects and coordinating with peers are required.

43 College Graduates Don't Always Out-Earn High School Grads, https://www.bloomberg.com/news/articles/2014-07-15/is-college-worth-it-some-high-school-grads-earn-more

The Student Path

The paths students take, even when seated at a desk, is a function of the movements they make. It can be as simple as what they put in their notebooks, how they turn the page of book, how they flip through their Facebook newsfeed, how they bob their head to music coming through their headphones, these movements are the result of conscious decisions based on years of adaptation. They learn in order to adapt their movements to the circumstances at that moment.

Bringing consciousness to even the slightest micro-movement brings imagination and curiosity into play to start the process of learning. The adaptations that can occur while a student is at an institution of higher education can only be described as remarkable.

Traditionally, learning outcomes are triggered through the act of reading and writing. For some, math proofs become a sequence of moves in which the student forms a pathway they use to solve an equation. The marks they make with a pencil on paper or in the sequence of keys struck on a keyboard become an art, a form of sketching.

With each keystroke or mark on a page, the student takes into account each letter and symbol they produce and how they sequence them to create meaning as words or formulas. They add words to shade the meanings to bring their intent into life in the form of sentences or steps to solve an equation.

What is done by the student in this way is also being done to them at the same time. If the student is asked to sit in a class-room and consume lectures, then they practice sitting. If they learn to make decisions merely as a result of a set of abstract calculations, they learn to devise "what if" scenarios without learning to identify problems as they develop. When they are encouraged to create copious notes, to sketch out their ideas for feedback from their peers, they open the door to a level of critical thinking beyond what is put in front of them to test their comprehension. Colleges need to help students go beyond what is known and safe, to imagine, to question, to experiment, in order to develop their unique voice, their professional identity.

The freedom to adapt, to imagine possibilities, to try things, to fail, to try again in a new way, has been discouraged in many undergraduate programs. Yet this is how we learn. When students fail a test in many colleges, often there is no chance for relearning and retaking that test. Without a solid grasp of the basics, students are left without the foundation they need to master what follows.

Colleges have increasingly focused on training students for careers in their fields of study, without asking students to study themselves in the process. In his watershed treatise published by American Scholar, William Deresiewicz depicted students at elite institutions as treated by different measures than those in other colleges. His subtitle speaks volumes by itself- "Our best universities have forgotten that the reason they exist is to make minds, not careers":

He describes the stereotype, "The way students are treated in college trains them for the social position they will occupy once they get out. At schools like Cleveland State, they're being trained for positions somewhere in the middle of the class system, in the depths of one bureaucracy or another. They're being conditioned for lives with few second chances, no extensions, little support, narrow opportunity—lives of subordination, supervision, and control, lives of deadlines, not guidelines. At places like Yale, of course, it's the reverse... Elite schools nurture excellence, but they also nurture what a former Yale graduate student I know calls "entitled mediocrity." A is the mark of excellence; A- is the mark of entitled mediocrity. It's another one of those metaphors, not so much a grade as a promise. It means, don't worry, we'll take care of you. You may not be all that good, but you're good enough." [44]

Contrast this with the stories in the Huffington Post by a recent college graduate, who took control of her own path and continues to discover new options as a blogger. Daphne Spyropoulos describes pursuing her passions across a cornucopia of domains:

[44] The Disadvantages of an Elite Education, https://theamericanscholar.org/the-disadvantages-of-an-elite-education/

"I would eavesdrop on my brother's pharmacology notes, I would attend ancient drama weekly conferences, I would create content for blogs, I would intern for international businesses and I would part time model for an agency close to my university classes."[45]

Rather than worry about her career as it relates to the expectations of others, she has learned that "life-thirst can show you incredible things." Daphne embraced college as a time for looking into anything of interest, for taking chances, even to live without purpose, to be foolish.

She, like other students who embrace their opportunities for higher education, has discovered her value goes beyond the things she accumulates or the money she receives. What she creates, how she shares it, and how people make use of it identifies who she is and her place in the world.

Daphne's are actively aware of their own social and reputational value as well. Her "assemblage of experiences" clearly create a sense of direction, regardless of what schools she attended. She exhibits a keen sense of what interests her, what she is good at and what others find of value. How she develops the intersection of these unique characteristics of herself promises to yield a life well lived, a life worth watching.

Because of the technology at their disposal, today's students wrestle with their unique experience in the world to find their place in it. They can travel widely to do this. They have the news and the knowledge of the universe at their fingertips. They engage in meaningful work. They discover colleagues and form lasting alliances. They embark on missions. Their

---

45 Advice For Unsettling University Graduates, http://www.huffingtonpost.com/daphne-c-spyropoulos/advice-for-unsettling-uni_b_8651480.html

higher education comes through these activities and how they make use of the tools and relationships they form. The higher education process literally augments reality.

The Fourth Industrial Revolution

When higher education is viewed as a process, to be practiced at any time, in any place, its institutional touch points take on new dimensions. In particular, the process of stepping beyond a circle of friends and family, of adapting to professional life, becomes a cultural imperative. As societal needs change, so should the process of guidance and education as they are applied to future generations of students.

Consider the three fundamental shifts in institutions of higher education: preparation for agrarian societies, the transition to industrial organizations and the emergence of "knowledge workers." The role of higher education continues to be frozen across centuries of cultural development.

Depending on the needs of society, students have been offered suggestions for how to live well based on what has worked in the past. In general, the sons and daughters of each current generation are always afforded the best opportunities imaginable by the generations that immediately precede them.[46]

In agrarian times, higher education was the exclusive domain of the elite classes. Typically, royal, religious and privileged families sought out tutors and counselors for their sons and daughters to address issues as they arose. Since that time, young students have been expected to acquire skills for use in later life. They developed their identities. They built alliances. They addressed challenges.

With prosperity came a need to cultivate the offspring of elite classes. Modern colleges were invented to broaden the reach of the most sought-after dons, counselors and tutors. The systems in place at Cambridge and the Ivy League still draw from this heritage. They continue to pass along elite status to new generations, even as layers of new leaders have emerged from outside traditional elite classes.

The Industrial Revolution brought with it the need for more informed decisions made by more people in positions of authority within independent enterprises. Fortunes were made by tycoons whose background was anything but elite. The children of these captains of industry fought for elite status but not without struggles. The world they were entering, of transportation, communications and commerce, did not map well to the elite professions of law, clergy and recitation

---

46 How Britain went from making things to sitting at a desk: Census reveals huge drop in people working in factories and farms, http://www.dailymail.co.uk/news/article-2336248/How-Britain-went-making-things-sitting-desk-Census-reveals-huge-drop-people-working-factories-farms.html

of the classics as they were taught in colleges. To develop the talents needed by society, a new kind of university emerged, from Rensselaer Polytechnic Institute to Carnegie Mellon and Stanford University. These focused on practical application of science in everyday life.

Practically speaking, farming communities across the United States saw trucks and tractors change their way of life. They saw the future for their children was no longer on the farm, but in factories. These factories included machine shops, offices and manufacturing all in one locations. Universities were established to develop engineers and factory managers. As industries transformed how people lived, the system of education featured the time clock, rows of desks or work benches and other characteristics of factory life.[47]

Colleges were essentially part of a "weeding out" process that facilitated talent selection. By this process, some outstanding young talent could be identified and provided a path to elite status. Promising students could aspire to managerial positions. Sophisticated enterprises required huge capital investments to bring all functions under one roof.[48]

The Second World War highlighted how increased coordination and communications fueled growth in large organizations. Mass communications created mass markets which enabled mass production. No longer did engineering, sales and service functions operate under the same roof as manufacturing and assembly lines.

Servicemen who had experience managing logistics by

47 Chevrolet Gear and Axle, https://www.marygrove.edu/academics/institutes/institute-for-detroit-studies/literary-map-of-detroit/item/11-chevrolet-gear-and-axle.html
48 Great Cutaway Drawing of Evening Star Building in 1922, http://ghostsofdc.org/2014/11/04/great-cutaway-drawing-evening-star-building-1922/

moving military divisions around the globe joined the work force as "knowledge workers." Many never set foot in factories. Offices became the predominant workplace. The in-box became the new time clock and the benchmark for measuring performance. And, with the advent of computers and networks, office work propelled international coordination, supply chains and distribution networks.[49]

Colleges grew not only to explore and grow academically- they churned out professionals across a spectrum of specialties in order to supply the needs of businesses, large and small. An academic degree signaled a certain amount of capacity and potential at a time when companies were willing to take the time needed to train and develop talent.

The world of work, of workers and workplaces has already changed almost beyond recognition when viewed from an "office" perspective. It is now mobile, global and creative. Work is done as needed, where needed. Alliances are formed and missions defined at a pace inconceivable using outdated mass-market, "command and control" parameters.

Higher education is called upon repeatedly as more professionals than ever live by their wits. Their imaginations become their biggest asset- not their upbringing, their brawn or their past achievements. Each enterprise can be defined as any coordinated project. The tools to support the enterprise are no longer fixed, which enables a return to heterogeneous working environments. Agriculture, health care, manufacturing, education: virtually all industries are becoming "smarter", enabled by intelligent devices as well as a highly-skilled worldwide

---

49 In it for the long haul: Number of Britons travelling three hours for work every day up by 50 per cent in five years, http://metro.co.uk/2013/05/16/in-it-for-the-long-haul-number-of-britons-travelling-3-hours-for-work-every-day-rises-50-in-5-years-3763036/

work force that may work remotely.

Driving this astonishing rate of change are the rapid development of new technologies and the impact of their adoption. The leading US private equities firm, Blackrock, with over \$4 trillion dollars under management, identifies the sweeping nature of the changing world our children are stepping into.[50] They point to three trends that support the increased importance of higher education, both within schools and in the wild:

Trend 1: The rate of new technologies is reaching saturation. It took air travel nearly 50 years before it became a ubiquitous service available to all. The same level of adoption has been achieved by smartphones in under 10 years.

Trend 2: Businesses are becoming more efficient through the application of new technologies. Among the top 1,500 US stocks over the past 35 years, those successfully managing their effective inventory levels to 0% has grown from 75 to over 300.

Trend 3: While automation is replacing workers in low-skill, highly-repetitive jobs, industries are seeking more highly-skilled, creative professionals. These adaptive, imaginative individuals will employ higher education throughout their careers, whether on their own, with their peers or with institutional assistance.

50 The Topic We Should All Be Paying Attention to (in 3 Charts), https://www.blackrock-blog.com/2015/12/11/economic-trends-in-charts/

New School Means Seeing the World in a New Way

New School students today must decide what path of inquiry to take, what to build, even who to include on a team. They learn to break down problems into their foundational elements. In a "new school" college environment students not only design projects and experiments, they design roles and recruit talent to take on the jobs to be done. They see the world in a different way when they can break it apart and put it back together using the resources they have at their disposal.

Traditional classrooms typically package what others have learned before. Students today have the capability to learn on their own by exercising their wits, their tools and their access to knowledge. But, they must learn to listen to each problem and its context as a design challenge in order to apply their resources effectively. They see things differently when they involve themselves in the multitude of choices involved in the design process itself.

At an introductory level, developing a feel for design sharpens student focus on what matters. As they progress, they must address the constraints and resources required to achieve goals. Most traditional college courses hide such design considerations when they package up assignments. For students to reach their potential, the college experience must afford them the privilege of experimentation in an environment where they feel safe to fail.

At an advanced level, tracking, measuring and assessing the forces that sustain or break a design, then iterating the design to accommodate real-world feedback, becomes the centerpiece for professional success. These students need to sharpen their ability to interrogate and speculate in a team setting. Together, they can develop hypotheses, design experiments, and set outcomes to measure. By putting scientific methods into practice throughout their academic careers, students are afforded the opportunity to determine where they fit in, to assess their own strengths and where they need to shore up their skills while they investigate new approaches.

Playing on a Big Stage

The adaptation required by the college experience, and repeated throughout life, is rooted in each person's desire to change, to make a difference and to learn along the way. When the goal is to improve, to perform as a pro, outcomes become tangible. They can be measured and have consequences. Students must be encouraged to develop new approaches to put themselves in the game, particularly as situations change. Higher education, whether in college or thereafter, provides the environment that makes adaptation possible. Gaining alignment is no small task for students who have never stepped outside of the expectations placed on them through "old school" traditions.

Students must be inspired to discover things they want to do together. They must play with new identities and find new roles in which they contribute to something that is larger than themselves. What they make of these things, how they bring their knowledge and skills to play in respect to what is in front of them as individuals and members of teams, sets the stage for their adaptation and their success as individuals as well. Successful "new school" environments provide opportunities that encourage their development through imagination, play and discovery.

We are now surrounded by expertise and knowledge. Students will check Google for additional insights when a textbook or teacher gets them to look at things in a new way. They compare themselves with their peers, yet need help asking for feedback. In traditional settings, they are accustomed to being shown the "right" answer. As they work collaboratively on teams, they must develop a new language to support their peers and yet challenge them to improve the overall performance of the group.

Melding Art and Science

"Old School" thinking often categorizes the arts into narrow niches while promoting "hard science." The black and white

75

nature of digital has recently been championed over the shades of grey that still distinguish our analog world. Almost universally, disciplines have been silo'd into their own buildings, their own campuses. What if higher education required nimbly melding art and science, task and flow, to every student's experience? Increasing evidence is surfacing to indicate this is necessary, more than ever, for adapting to new ideas and ambiguous situations that don't have past road maps to follow.

Ultimately, colleges respond to the needs of the time. When the cultural goal of higher education was to ease the transition from farm work to factory work, the task was to get students to show up and perform on time. The creative elements of factory work was in the up-front design processes.

When the cultural goal of higher education was to promote the transition of factory workers into office work, the task was to cultivate "knowledge." The specializations of office departments is replicated throughout most college curricula and cultures. The design of organizations, their models of operation and the systems used to sustain them reflect the "command and control" methods honed in military organizations. Work and class experiences replicated the dictates of the "in-box."

Today, we experience dynamic change in the world and in work. No longer is there one "in-box" to work from, there are many. Students can expect to be employed by dozens of different organizations over their careers. Today's organizations are dynamic, regularly restructuring and redefining themselves as they adapt to global supply and market issues.

Preparing students for this increasingly mobile world, and often a "gig-economy", requires being able to solve problems that may have never existed before as a central aspect of higher education. Students must both calculate and flow in the world they will work in. To remain relevant colleges must foster knowledge and skills as well as performance and disposition.

Bringing Artists and Scientists Together

A recent *New Yorker* article asks the question: Can video games help stroke victims?[51] It details new possibilities for stroke patients with impaired arms. "Using a robotic sling, patients learn to sync the movements of their arms to the leaping, diving dolphin; that motoric empathy... will keep patients engaged in the immersive world of the game for hours, contracting their real muscles to move the virtual dolphin."

The astounding result is that strokes might no longer be viewed as catastrophic events anymore than a ruptured ACL is now. That these might be treated by non-invasive methods promises to remove strokes as the #1 cause of long-term disability in the US, effecting as much as the nearly 1 million incidents each year. How this new therapy might apply to student learning might change the lives of many millions more.

The Johns Hopkins Medicine facility run by the Department of Neurology featured in the article is named the Brain, Learning, Animation, and Movement (BLAM) lab.[52] They describe the opportunity they face: "We believe the time is ripe for a new fusion between academia and industry ... Neuroscience innovations seamlessly translated into highly lucrative

---

51 HELPING HAND: Robots, video games, and a radical new approach to treating stroke patients. http://www.newyorker.com/magazine/2015/11/23/helping-hand-annals-of-medicine-karen-russell
52 Brain, Learning, Animation, and Movement Lab, http://blam-lab.org/

products in the entertainment industry (have) the capacity to self-fund on the order of hundreds of millions... Johns Hopkins has the unique opportunity to rival MIT and Stanford in bridging two worlds that should no longer be kept apart in biomedical science."

At the root of their method is to educe movement by patients through immersion in and interaction with "Pixar-level" animations. John Krakauer, the Director of the BLAM 123lab, describes what happens with stroke patients in current hospital environments.

What he describes has relevance to a discussion about what happens in higher education. The theme he hammers home, which he hopes his audience takes away, cannot be understated. "You really need to bring artists and scientists together."

"We have this window, and we are not using it", he says. It turns out that mice recover from strokes if you give immediate training feedback. He shows how there is a special time period in which the brain is highly active within moments after a stroke event, which provides an opportunity to adapt and develop new pathways to regain full function. The ideal scenario is to put mice into "enriched environments":[53]

"You put them in with their friends. You give them toys", he says. Providing a "fair ground environment" leads to increased levels of motivation, reward, interaction, enjoyment and fun in which mice recover completely without receiving task-specific training.

His experiments provide evidence that environments which foster enjoyment, play and experimentation improve recovery. After his team developed a video game environment supported

---

53 A critical window for recovery after stroke, https://www.youtube.com/watch?v=Sjkg-m6x3LlY

by an exo-skeletal system that enabled human stroke patients to extend their arms over a wide range of motion, he was astonished by the delight exhibited by his first test subjects. "We are very hopeful that we will bring fun and play back into the brain injury recovery environment", says Krakauer. The interactive experience of being a dolphin engaged in an undersea shark battle forces patients to exercise, to adapt and to learn at a very deep level. "The ability to be in a controlling environment...is unbelievably pleasurable."

While these are fascinating and revolutionary advances, teamwork between talented people from unexpected disciplines was required to develop these new training mechanisms. Krakauer suggests computer scientists should work with animation artists and robotics experts in order to develop the systems that can effect motion, adaptation and learning at this level. His trans-disciplinary team works "cheek to jowl" with neuroscientists, clinicians and therapists. He says, "You have to bring people together who at first blush you may not think should be in the same room."

The Intersection of Creativity and Technology

If institutions of higher learning are designed to prepare future generations for the world, then the traditional "old school" college experience must adapt. Does a curriculum designed to produce graduates for often outdated professions make sense for an increasingly mobile work force? The answer is a resounding "NO." Quite literally, once self-driving cars become viable, people will be working and learning in the down time that is currently wasted when their hands are on the wheel.

Higher education has always been about using available technologies to do what is needed by society. Our society has moved on from traditional ways. It is past the time to rethink what we offer and the learning environments we create. We are already late to the game and employers recognize it.

In the world we live in today, the meteoric rise of services like Wikipedia (media), Kickstarter (finance), Uber (transportation) and AirBnB (housing) illustrate the speed of self-organizing economics. Higher education must empower students to shoulder the responsibility to design and build in order to learn, no matter their course of study. In this process, the higher order of coordination, teamwork and communications made possible with networked technologies opens the doors to new ways of life, increased understanding and unprecedented levels of problem-solving. Students, whether in school or on their own, will leverage a staggering array of new technologies to build that future.

Culture of Makers

Something fundamental happens when students are asked to view games from a "make" perspective.[54] Challenged with the task of building one of their own in the classroom, students must first deconstruct their own experience of a game. They must then reduce it to the basic fundamentals. They need to delve into probabilities, evaluate the balance of chance vs skill from a design perspective. They recognize the need for programming physics engines to provide a realistic feel to their game. They must consider who will play the game and and anticipate what they will feel, not just what they will do.

---

54 This Is Why Making Your Own Video Games Leads To Quality Learning, http://www.forbes.com/sites/jordanshapiro/2016/04/09/this-is-why-making-your-own-video-games-leads-to-quality-learning/#368922717868

In the process of making something like a video game, students must shift their perspective and apply their imaginations in powerful new ways. They speculate to think through what can exist in "makeable" new worlds. They must construct imaginative experiments to test their concepts in order to bring that world into reality. They play freely with the options, imagining the flow of play unhindered by physical impediments. Then, as they discover the very real resource constraints, they turn on their imaginative skills as they seek innovative solutions. They form teams. They embark on missions. They assemble the code, art and sound assets that bring their work to life. Together, they bring themselves to the team in order to accomplish a goal. They stand up to the challenges inherent in what they are trying to accomplish and apply their skills for the benefit of the team. They deep dive and mentor each other. They see what they have created and how it affects others. Through new kinds of classes, club and independent activities, students prepare in a way that more likely matches what is needed by the companies that want to hire talent for their organizations.[55]

The values that surface through experiential learning are not exclusive to game programming. Making apps, animated films and video games can reignite interest in just about any field of study. To be believable, characters should wear clothing that accurately reflects their historical and economic status within a given period of time. Movements should follow the laws of physics. Sounds must convey an experience with meaningful authenticity (the crunch of a footstep on gravel should reflect the psychological condition of a character in that moment).

---

55 Industrial Strength Graduates and Commercially Viable Apps, http://dx.doi.org/10.3998/3336451.0017.303

Developing Common Language

Agile development processes have evolved into business practice and can be adapted for class uses as well. "Rapid prototyping" methods challenge teams to develop a common language across the vastly different objectives of the Business Analyst, the Product Development team and the Quality Assurance needs of the group.[56] Students can take roles as a team investigates their approach to a problem, develops a strategy for solving it, and then execute together to produce something they can all be proud of. The terminology of the scrum, the sprint and the pivot evoke the level of commitment and effort required for projects to succeed, whether in industry or educational arenas.

Startup entrepreneurs must adapt to changing circumstances, to match learning a required skill against sometimes dramatic consequences. It's not something you can "Google," read about in a textbook, or take a test to gauge your learning and then get a grade that has relevance in the real world. Contributing to a team goes beyond a conceptual understanding and is as important as the knowledge gained through the classroom. Every detail is important.

The habits learned by trial and error are what will serve as a foundation for a career and a lifetime.[57] When students learn to get in the game, whether it is in sports or in a team project or entrepreneurial effort, all play vital roles in learning adaptation for emerging new ecosystems, and the sky is the limit.

Playing essential roles in discovery and innovation, startups

56 Introducing the Three Amigos, https://www.scrumalliance.org/community/articles/2013/2013-april/introducing-the-three-amigos
57 How Running A Startup Taught Me More Than School Ever Could, http://www.forbes.com/sites/rajatbhageria/2015/09/14/how-running-a-startup-taught-me-more-than-school-ever-could/#537ad6d965d7

and/or sports teams inform the pathfinding and career choices that lie ahead. Trying out new roles brings with it new perspectives in which to gain deeper appreciation. Taking on more senior roles enables advanced students the opportunity to mentor or supervise others on their team. The explosive growth of project-based learning indicates some of what is possible across a growing spectrum of college experiences. This, too, is part of the "new school" approach.

Machines Work, Networks Play

How do colleges and universities provide the best possible adaptation model for becoming a professional and lifelong learner? Critics have emerged to offer powerful analysis of the current model. William Deresiewicz, the author of "Excellent Sheep", has ignited a firestorm at some universities with his criticisms. While he offers no solutions, he cries out for a shift to a more fluid and personal exposure to life outside of college, to mobilize the talents of students across all strata of society.[58]

He suggests students offer far more than they are asked to reveal during their academic careers. He is struck by students and parents who invest their resources trying to do a million things to meet the expectations of others. He suggests they delve more deeply, to commit themselves to their own higher education. He puts his finger on the issue that students are the ones who must learn, who must perform, who must adapt in order to achieve.

He says, "Each individual student has a choice. You didn't have a choice when you were 11, but now you do. Even though

---

58 Bill Deresiewicz: "Are Stanford Students Just (Really Excellent) Sheep?" https://www.youtube.com/watch?v=DKVLf7X4zSQ

the chance of changing institutional structures is small, it's worth trying. You can decide to not follow the direction that your training has sent you in."

In other words, students need to figure things out for themselves. And the best way to figure things out was thought to be in a classroom, the library, the athletic field. These, after all, are where traditional colleges and universities have invested their resources.

In "College Disrupted", Ryan Craig describes college priorities in terms of the 4Rs: research, ratings, real estate, and rah-rah (football and branded sports). In the traditional college model, students pay for their education, with very little accounting for their competencies, beyond a grade point average. A college degree, he suggests, is a weak proxy for the achievements that are sought after by employers. He suggests that services like LinkedIn will soon automatically match competencies described in user profiles with job postings.

On LinkedIn, outsourced recruitment services do the match-making and derive revenue by successfully placing candidates at hiring institutions. Craig suggests we are not far away from educational institutions being paid primarily from placement fees, rather than tuition.[59]

Outside of traditional colleges and universities, non-accredited "boot camps" have sprung up to help retrain and retool college graduates for the kinds of careers provided by today's growth organizations. They have the task of convincing potential students, many of whom have degrees, jobs and families, to quit working at what they were doing for 3-6 months, pay thousands of dollars, and get on the fast track. Increasingly,

---

59 College Disrupted: The Great Unbundling of Higher Education, http://livestream.com/asugsvsummit/events/3914367/videos/83151866

they are moving toward both immersive and online experiences with the potential for employers to sponsor learning experiences.

Udacity's innovative nanodegree programs are another step in this direction. Their curriculum for Android developers is very low priced, but yields critical signals to employers, who then pay for access to the best students and nanodegree holders.[60]

The work world they depict can hardly be described as an office, a factory, a building or machine. It is a world of dynamic networks. Designing these, playing in them, and providing services through them describes the employment opportunities that have been largely unmet by traditional colleges and universities.

"The next billion people coming online will interact with the Internet for the very first time using only a mobile device. There are so many people who are consumers of technology, but it's so much more powerful to be a creator of technology. Everyone has unique experiences and strengths. They can draw on that and use that to identify problems in their community. They can then use technology to solve them. You can imagine something that you think should exist and you can actually go and build it."

What is known as the Maker movement illustrates the growing interest of people around the world to move from being passive users to active creators.[61] Two new college programs that embrace a "maker" orientation are the Stanford d School and the Jimmy Iovine and Andre Young Academy at USC.

Technology-enhanced work such as this cries out for

60 Android Developer Nanodegree, https://www.udacity.com/course/android-developer-nanodegree--nd801
61 Why the Maker Movement Is Important to America's Future, http://time.com/104210/maker-faire-maker-movement/

accredited institutional support. It is not about completing assigned work, but about imagining something new and then going about the tasks required to bring it to life. This describes industrialization at an individual, self-directed level. Far beyond coming to grips with the ideas of those who have come before, this new view embraces each individual as capable of joining others, bringing their knowledge, skills and passions to life through collaboration in order to make an impact.

In the Flow State

Todd Richmond is head of the Advanced Prototypes Group at the USC Institute for Creative Technologies. He breaks the challenge down to very simple terms: the analog world and the digital are like mixing oil and vinegar. They are emulsional, meaning they don't adhere to each other easily. He is exploring the very analog relationship of humans and what gets left out when they become digital.[62]

"Analog sound waves are reproduced most of the time now by digital means, which means by zeros and ones", he said at TEDxVeniceBeach in 2013. "This means we take a continuous motion and turn it into stair-steps... Humans, on the other hand, are incredibly nuanced. The thing that humans do very well is to pick up on subtle variations around them."[63] He has basically described what should be taught in college.

---

62 emulsion - a two phase system that is immiscible, http://emulsionalworld.com/
63 Analog soul - digital world: Todd Richmond at TEDxVeniceBeach, https://www.youtube.com/watch?v=O2rl0SNt3oM

Perhaps most important for college students are their skills of observation and listening. Stressed out college students who are continually tested for their comprehension take on a "deer in the headlights" posture: always alert to whatever log they must jump over next. "New school" students become immersed, they develop a sense of mission. They learn to commit themselves wholeheartedly to a common purpose with their team. They listen deeply in order to decode the messages they receive and to discern meaning out of the fragments of data they are working with. The behaviors they notice in those around them, illuminated by critiques, the roles they take on and the challenges of bringing projects to life, help "new school" students to recognize opportunities that others might ignore.

Another musician-scientist is Daniel Levitin, a neuroscientist at McGill University. When interviewed about his book, Information Overload, he talks about the decision fatigue that comes from too many task-oriented processes that most students encounter during a day at college. "Every time you make a decision, whether it's a trivial one or an important one, it uses up just about the same amount of nutrients.

"The cells doing the work use up about the same amount of metabolic activity. Also, there's a biological cost of switching from one thing to the next. It depletes neural resources which you need in order to stay focused." He talks abut the antidote to decision fatigue, which is what he calls "daydreaming mode." He recommends students and professionals alike should let their minds wander more, which exerts a natural pull on our consciousness. "Our brain knows that it needs that antidote, as a sort of a reset button. When your brain has a chance to wander for a few minutes you can come back to the task refreshed."[64]

Levitin has hooked up famous musicians such as Sting to brain scanners while they compose music, the epitome of a compositional task. He's also studied the scans of jazz musicians as they improvise and found their brain activity shuts down to allow their actions to flow. "Whether you are an acrobat, a computer programmer, an athlete, or a painter, you don't reach the flow state until you have mastered the fundamentals.

"In the flow state, you don't have to think about what you are doing. Something takes over. You see this in a transcendent performance in any domain. An actor who disappears into a role isn't thinking, 'I'll put my right foot here, and I'm standing at a bar, so I'd better put my hand on the counter now.'"[65]

This mixing of task and flow was also described in Ken Kesey's collaborative novel written by his University of Oregon students. "The trick is for us to build character in our characters," Kesey said, "to breathe life into them, to get them to stand up, stretch and start doing stuff. We're not interested in pulling strings, in being puppeteers. We want these people to rise up off the page. Then we sit back and follow them through the novel."[66]

The total immersion reflected in the novel writing can be replicated across a spectrum of the college curriculum. In a sculpture class, for instance, it is helpful to include the study of écorché, a painting or sculpture of a human figure with the skin removed to display the musculature. Students develop

---

64 Information Overload, https://www.youtube.com/watch?v=L8y50TXSE4s
65 Understanding the Musical Brain, https://www.berklee.edu/berklee-today/fall-2015/daniel-levitin
66 http://www.rollingstone.com/culture/features/ken-keseys-eclectic-writing-ac-id-test-19891005

their initial characters and then peel back the skin to reveal sinew, muscle and skeleton. Through this exercise, characters take on new dimensions. Stories can be developed around each character based on their structure, balance and physiognomy. Explaining how a character lives in the world, their history and path, informs the work done by others on collaborative teams.

The same can be said for UX (user experience) design. Students in teams work together to identify sets of characters who might use a product or service. By working closely together, they develop the characters and the roles they play in working toward a common goal. From these, scenarios emerge, similar to the plot of a novel. This is a basis of "design thinking", the discipline refined at Stanford's d-School.[67] It is a form of cultural anthropology that is taking on new life in collaborative, project-oriented, student designed college classes.

---

67 Stanford University Institute of Design, http://dschool.stanford.edu/

Of Sketches, Compositions and Flow

The guidance afforded students in college environments becomes critical as the world becomes more dynamic. Innovations in high-technology have changed the game in colleges across the country and the world. Many of these are digital, from the cloud to sensor to device. They are mobile, in that college students and professionals carry them wherever they go. And they are social in the way people can reach out, connect and associate more freely than ever imagined.

However, these personal computing capabilities have not been altogether accepted and have been even banned in classrooms and in colleges around the world. The "Old School" way was to isolate each student, to restrict their movements to sitting at a desk with prescribed learning materials in front of them, and to test them on their ability to retain whatever information was deemed most relevant within some canonical constraint.

Contrary to older methods, "New School" methods embrace the student experience as they journey through unfamiliar territory. Their observational skills, how they reach out to bring in resources, how they make sense of what they have assembled, and how they compose themselves in order to create something extraordinary, are all measurable achievements. Knowledge itself becomes secondary.

By drawing out the capabilities of students through meaningful activities and collaborations they can take with them into their professional lives, adaptation is more rapid as they take on the world around them with fresh eyes.

Today's students use the devices in their pockets to document what they eat, what they see and how they feel. With a bit of imagination, they search Google, YouTube, Khan Academy, TED talks and Wikipedia to come up to speed quickly in virtually any subject area they wish to explore. They binge: exploring simulations, scholarly works and breaking news across a staggering spectrum of interests.

Adaptive, formative assessments might sound plausible when examined from an "old school" context. The emergence of "robot tutor" systems like Knewton promise to guide students through one learning exercise to another, based on what they need to learn.[68] These become secondary when viewed from the "new school" perspective.

The society of the future requires students who are capable and ready to do things, to make things and to make a

---

68 This Robot Tutor Will Make Personalizing Education Easy, http://www.wired.com/2015/08/knewton-robot-tutor/

difference. They need to adapt to the world around them, to get their hands dirty, to form teams and receive direct feedback based on what they accomplish together.

Today's students create as well as consume. Students need to be involved in large projects in which they coordinate with others to create things larger in scope than they could have imagined on their own. In the past, this aspect of higher education has been almost impossible to manage, so it has been purged from the experience of many students. Classroom exercises have known outcomes in the "old school" way.

What is creativity and how do we assess its value? Certainly, no multiple-choice quiz or short essay can suffice. "New school" thinking welcomes students to try and fail until they find something they can work with. They claw their way through perspectives, approaches, technologies and roles. Their resilience and imagination surfaces when forced to adapt to the challenges they face grappling with a problem worth solving. It is when they make something together that their creativity can surface in meaningful ways for others to see. The process of making- the conceptualizing, sketching and pitching ideas, the early prototyping, the early experiments and failures, the feedback from others and ultimately the satisfaction that comes with playing a role in something bigger than self takes creativity beyond the isolated kind of activity most people associate with the concept of creativity.

Above all else, today's students are social beyond any earlier generation. They already have networks of friends and resources they interact with regularly outside of those in a classroom at a given period of time. They recruit others to join them in projects. They form alliances. They embark on missions. It is this aspect of "new school" that holds the promise that higher education can reach every student, regardless of heritage of the institution.

In many traditional structures, the very important work of real-world hypothesis development, experiment design and project management has been left to graduate students and research administrators. The recent explosion of entrepreneurial courses and other student-led projects reveals the immense resource being ignored across college student bodies. Not only can students develop their own missions while in college, it is critical that they do so in order to participate in the world after graduation, when they have no school support around them.

Practice, Practice, Practice

S tudents who practice in college what they will do thereafter can step in and perform as professionals upon graduation. They have developed their capacity to communicate, to work through problems and to commit themselves
fully to whatever mission they choose to serve. For them,
college is not something they leave behind, but something they
take with them. An elite college education, therefore, is what
enables graduates to participate fully in their local ecosystems,
at least in theory.

Ask students at the top flight institutions how much of their
time is spent going to lectures and how much time they spend
working on their own, team-oriented projects. The naturally
occurring networks on these campuses are apt to have better
funded and prepared students who are also better connected to

the world beyond college. As a result, these institutions provide more opportunities for undergraduates to pursue a graduate-education model, to work on real-world problems.

A significant number of graduates from elite institutions become highly successful in their post-graduate endeavors. Jonathan Wai, a research scientist at Duke University's Talent Identification Program, found that about 40% of the world's billionaires and corporate CEOs came from elite institutions. But, this means that over 60% of today's billionaires did not attend an elite institution.[69] We predict that number will to grow as colleges move to embrace new school methods.

---

69 A Shocking Number Of The World's Rich And Powerful Attended Elite Colleges, http://www.businessinsider.com/how-many-rich-powerful-people-went-to-elite-colleges-2014-6

Feedback and Critiques

L earning to give and receive feedback can be taught through the use of presentations and critiques: skills that are rarely a part of the "old school" college curricula. When students form teams and work on projects, presentations and performances become a central part of the college experience. In order to make these more meaningful, the active participation of the entire class in the form of critiques helps students find their comfort zone.

Offering critiques, and receiving them, warrants careful consideration as colleges adapt to the "new school" programs. Long established as the "signature" pedagogy in art and architecture, the critique method may be applied across a range of disciplines. Critique does not mean analysis and criticism. It is a foundational skill to communicate what one sees. Students must do it to learn it. Along the way, they learn to appreciate other points of view. Critiques are what move projects beyond "show and tell" into exercises of transformation. They move design beyond "design thinking" and stimulate iterations and adaptations. A myriad of academic activities can be improved using critiques to engage students in the assessment of:

- Writing assignments
- Thesis statements
- Presentations
- Role Playing
- Performances
- Clinical procedures and demonstrations
- Interviews
- Business plans

Stanford's Richard Reis has written a book called Tomorrow's Professor in which he includes helpful tips for academics wishing to further their teaching careers. He stresses the importance of students learning the etiquette required to make critique sessions successful.[70]

Reis says, "Most students do not have a lot of experience providing or receiving constructive criticism. Establishing proper etiquette and expectations for students can promote community, encourage participation, curb undesirable behavior, and help students understand their role in the critique process. Critique etiquette can either be presented by the instructor or created collaboratively by the class as a community building activity. Either way, clearly outlining students' roles

---

70 Tomorrow's Professor Postings, https://tomprof.stanford.edu/book

as both receiving a critique from peers, as well as providing a critique to peers fosters trust between students and helps them feel safe enough to take risks."[71]

The magic fostered by frequent critique sessions, not as a test at the end of a course, enables students to see their work from various points of view. They benefit from what college has to offer in ways that go deeper than the subject matter at hand. Their engagement with each other can develop along with their commitment to their pursuit of their college degree.

---

71 Teaching Through Critique: An Extra-Disciplinary Approach, https://tomprof.stan-ford.edu/posting/1406

Iterations, Reworking and Fine-Tuning

Coming up with a good idea (or coming up with the "right answer") can be quick and easy. Figuring out what to do with what has been learned, and then making something with it, making things happen, is where students benefit most. Deconstruction is as important as construction. Decoding is as important as coding. Learning fundamentals at a very deep level requires practice and communications between students.

Design emerges through evolutionary practice, as it always has. The iterations students put their projects through is a real-world testing process. Developing their capacity to question each other, the world around them and their own work expands their knowledge and opens their eyes to new possibilities. It also enables them to define themselves, their abilities and how they might contribute to the world as it changes. Perseverance is their key to success.

The art of dialog and critique, at the core of the higher education experience, lays the groundwork for iterative design and student success. It encourages them to speculate, to exercise their pragmatic imagination and to adapt to feedback. "Getting it right" goes far beyond submitting the right answers when quizzed. Old School thinking does a disservice to students when the approach to higher education is only experienced as an exchange of what you know rather than a free flow of imaginations, an unlocking of potential, a resetting of expectations.

By addressing a problem in a multitude of ways, of reworking a project until it takes on a life of its own, students experience a sense of agency through the habits they form. They take responsibility for their work. They set standards for themselves and those around them. In the end, their observations are what they offer others. Their viewpoints matter, particularly when mentoring their peers. Bringing their unique perspectives with them are as valuable as they skills learn along the way.

When students have the opportunity to work so closely together, friendships form and students prioritize their shared interests. They connect to the world through each other. In the process they take responsibility for their learning. They spend free time together. They create their own environment. It can seem like they are sitting around a camp fire, swapping stories, sharing dreams and reflecting on life.

For whatever reason, many colleges often relegate the social aspects of campus life to sports, recreation and parties. For today's connected and mobile students, building lasting relationships is perhaps the most important part of their learning process. The trust and openness students develop with their peers as they work together on projects sets the foundation for building effective relationships in the future.

New School Portfolios

Resumes are old school. Every college course should be developed such that students can put what they have learned into a portfolio that they can take with them upon graduations. The portfolio goes beyond tests they may have taken or papers they may have written. It is evidence of their learning. For example, hiring managers today want to see GitHub repositories when they hire technical engineers. They want to see evidence of a candidate's work because they are comparing students from college against those who are retooling their skill set through bootcamps or after a few years in the work force already.

Students without an online footprint are at a disadvantage. While in college, they should be saving and publishing their best work in whatever form is appropriate. An artist or designer without a demo reel will not be considered for work at the kind of company they dream of. No news organization will hire a student without seeing their blog or contributions to online publications. No venture capitalist will invest in a student project unless they see a track record on a site like Kickstarter. Student presentations at college should be designed so they result in portfolio quality materials.

New School colleges provide students the best possible platform with which to develop their portfolio. By working with teams, by mixing art, engineering and leadership talents throughout college, students can point to professional-grade work and describe their role within complex production pipelines.

All colleges should actively seek out industry advisors and mentors to identify what kinds of portfolios match their curriculum and design courses expressly for portfolio preparation. As an example, Texas A&M runs a summer Visualization program for graduate students in conjunction with Dreamworks animation.[72] Teams of students are challenged to develop storylines around a simple subject and then produce a 30-second animated short video. Dreamworks personnel give students critiques of their work throughout the process of the computer generated imaging production pipeline: pre-visualization, rigging, animation, surfacing, effects, lighting and rendering. The resulting portfolio artifacts are regularly celebrated at industry trade shows as well as supporting student candidacy within the industry upon graduation.

In addition to specific portfolio courses, the degree plans

---

72 Summer Animation Course with DreamWorks, http://viz.arch.tamu.edu/about/news/2012/8/23/summer-animation-course-dreamworks/

offered by colleges should contain portfolio opportunities across the curriculum. Students are energized by creating quality work that can be published, particularly as part of teams. The old school model of submitting work to faculty for comment and grading must evolve so that every student has the opportunity to see professional grade work developed and critiqued by their peers.

End-of-term team presentations take on even more meaning when visitors are invited into the class. An observer is privileged to see how less-prepared students are supported by their stronger peers. Projects take on a life that inspires deep dives into academic and scientific research which in turn brings out the best in every individual on the team. Learning is an evolutionary process as students grapple with their own talents and voice and appreciate their roles on teams.

Through such portfolio-related courses, students are challenged to expand their own capacity. They discover they can do more than they ever imagined on their own. They are inspired by their own classmates as well the mentors and experts they pull into their projects. Throughout their college years, they can focus on cultivating the unique values and practices that will actualize their potential.

Colleges are uniquely qualified to provide the enriched learning environment students need to break out into their own. Never before has such adaptation been supported by free or inexpensive resources. No longer is knowledge the province of a privileged few. No longer is technology so expensive or inaccessible that the resources required render it beyond reach or imagining. No longer does intimate contact with global communities require extensive travel and permissions for access. In short, all students today have the tools and resources they need to put their own ideas into play on a world stage. It is all about how we as institutions design and encourage learning.

New School Simulates the Real World

Current research reveals that students decide to go to college primarily to improve their employment opportunities, i.e., to get a job.[73] They look to colleges to prepare them not only to work in traditional jobs, but to also prepare them for a world that is changing beyond description. They are more aware that narrowly defined silos of academic disciplines may not help as much as acquiring useful skills and the disposition to put them to effective use.

Degrees in the humanities and social sciences have long served to prepare students for life after college. Enlightening students to the works of masters, exposing them to the thinking behind great accomplishments, underpins much of the current college curriculum. These degrees become even more valuable when students engage in hands-on experiences, work as teams and tackle real-world projects to apply what they learn in meaningful ways. The goal, then, is not just to "Let There Be Light" (or "Fiat Lux", UC Berkeley's famous motto), but to help students see more acutely, to see what others fail to see, and to bring their perspective to bear on the problems at hand, in real time. This practice enables them to see the picture, to imagine and pursue bigger things.

Self-actualization has long been at the pinnacle of psychologist Abraham Maslow's famous hierarchy of human needs.

73 2015 COLLEGE DECISIONS SURVEY: PART I, http://dev-edcentral.pantheonsite.io/wp-content/uploads/2015/05/FINAL-College-Decisions-Survey-528.pdf

Colleges are increasingly demonstrating how important the actualization process is. A startup launched in a dorm room, for example, illustrates how students might mix imagination, skills and industriousness to innovate and adapt. This process of actualization should be a central theme across all college campuses, resulting in quality preparation for personal and professional achievements beyond what has been largely practiced in the past.

College as Simulators

How can colleges, then, function as simulators in which students experience the various possibilities afforded them fueled by their sense of who they are, their skills and their ability to work with others? This should be at the core of the college experience. Students must practice in college what they will do on the job.

On their own, without formal education, students can apply readily available technology and form teams to address problems large and small. They can share resources across disciplines, outside the structure of the university itself. They can "deep dive" into areas of interest that spring up through the projects they take on. In this way, "new school" students customize their education while at the same time they follow the prescriptions required to attain their college degree.

With the internet at our fingertips, research can happen anywhere. Increasingly, real-time data flows are becoming available globally. Science and innovation are being advanced outside the structures of academic hierarchies. Unburdened by old notions of structure and tradition, enterprising undergrads can be encouraged to research, file patents, start new businesses, even become leaders in new fields they create. Traditional rigor applied to new opportunities provides students with the scaffolding to help them succeed. Colleges that have not yet come to this realization need to catch up and, as cultures of learning, are ideally positioned to do so.

At the primary and secondary levels, schools are adapting and some are more innovative than many colleges. A parent says about her daughter's experience in Palo Alto, the very well-heeled community surrounding Stanford, "Malina's teacher has provided parents with a password for an app that teaches kindergartners the basic principles of Java using a game. She loves this app. She plays it at home in the afternoon. The after-school program offers—for a fee—training in coding, design thinking and 3-D printing."[74] Similar stories are surfacing in communities across the country.

What if teachers embrace the use of technology to develop the apps, games and the talent of each student? Consider video games, for example. Most students love them because they are fun. They use them to build operational skills and develop their sense of strategic decision making. They use them to deep dive into characters, plot and drama. We have reached a point now where parents use games regularly too, and even play with their children.[75] It is time to embrace the video game as an educational tool that leads to quality learning. Making video games develops transferrable skill sets like decision making, teamwork, problem solving, creative thinking, empathy

---

74 Guest Opinion: Want to understand Silicon Valley? Send your kid to a Palo Alto school, http://www.paloaltoonline.com/news/2016/05/28/guest-opinion-want-to-understand-silicon-valley-send-your-kid-to-a-palo-alto-school
75 Should Parents Play Videogames With Their Children? http://www.wsj.com/articles/should-parents-play-videogames-with-their-children-1441899567

and failure tolerance. At the college level, the growth of Game Development programs supports the educational advantages of this approach, taking into account the academics, skills and career value inherent in the process of making games.[76]

Harnessing Imaginations

While colleges have done a remarkable job developing the resources needed for scientific research and industry, the challenge of simulating the world through what has been wired in the past decades will require a quantum leap in preparation. A wider appreciation of the research, such as that produced at UCLA by the team led by Shelley E. Taylor in 1998 in their paper "Harnessing the Imagination: Mental Simulation, Self-Regulation and Coping" deserves careful examination.[77] As tools for measuring performance evolve, fitness trackers will be revealing brain and bio mechanical activity as well.

In a TED talk in 2008, Christopher DeCharms described potential medical benefits of viewing functional MRI data in real time by patients themselves, who can then self-regulate, develop new neural pathways and imagine new possibilities.[78] With the rapid advancement of imaging technologies, our children may well grow up with mirrors that show their brain functions. Given advances like this, preparing students for the future goes beyond lectures, books and tests.

---

76 The Princeton Review Ranks Top 50 Undergrad & Top 25 Grad Schools to Study Game Design for 2016, http://www.princetonreview.com/press/game-design-press-release

77 Harnessing the Imagination, http://icds.uoregon.edu/wp-content/uploads/2013/03/Harnessing-the-Imagination-Mental-Simulation-Self-regulation-and-Coping.pdf

78 A look inside the brain in real time, https://www.ted.com/talks/christopher_decharms_scans_the_brain_in_real_time

John Seely Brown and Ann Pendleton-Jullian have constructed a framework that describes a spectrum of imagination, from the concrete world of perception and reasoning to a more fluid basis for innovation based on speculation, experimentation and free play. What they point to is supported by recent developments like the one DeCharms describes.

Colleges have the unique potential to radically affect the trajectories of billions of people. With a "new school" approach to higher education, institutions can examine the goals and perceived benefits of what they offer. Only by doing so, will they remain relevant with this rapidly changing world.

The interplay between students and how they adapt with each other within their physical environment forms the basis for higher education. Think of it as a cultural petri dish where all manner of things are being developed and formed, new perceptions are being explored with colleagues and new endeavors are being put into play. From this perspective, cultivating imaginations in order to adapt to a world in constant change takes center stage.[79]

79 A New Culture of Learning: Cultivating the Imagination for a World of Constant Change http://www.newcultureoflearning.com/

What survives and flourishes brings with it growth. New life forms are generated, if only temporarily. Learning is a byproduct of the process. Students become adapt at playing new roles, working with new peers and new tools to affect outcomes together. As an example of this concept in action, entrepreneurship programs are taking hold around the world. One experienced teacher describes the accelerated startup as the new business school.[80]

The Mixing Experience

Of course, only a fraction of those who play baseball in college go on to become professional baseball players. However, the mixing provided by athletic team activities is valuable by itself. Students develop a "can do" attitude on athletic fields that accompanies them on the paths they choose and with the people they choose to meet along the way. This mixing experience consequently develops a sense of agency and helps students adapt and achieve long after their college days are over.

Colleges must cultivate this sense of agency in order for their graduates to operate more effectively in the wild. But, schools don't need athletic teams to breed agency within their students. Study groups, clubs, incubators, meetups, hackathons and internships afford students opportunities to become involved with each other and with professionals while they are in college.

Another New School approach, entrepreneurial thinking, motivates students to go beyond classroom learning. Some even start businesses while in school. Stories abound of large

---

80 Accelerated Startup – The New Business School, https://www.inkshares.com/books/accelerated-startup-the-new-business-school

companies that started in college dorm rooms, such as Dell and Facebook. Perhaps due to these examples, entrepreneurial programs are being replicated in business classrooms around the world.

The rigors of running a startup company has become a more common experience across college campuses. Students can "pitch" their homework or project ideas hackathon style. Students can "scrum" or "huddle" together regularly as they work on projects, to become familiar with sharing progress updates and coordinating next steps. They can form short term goals and "sprint" to accomplish milestones together to push forward within longer term project goals. As their projects evolve, student teams learn to "pivot", or move in a new direction when their hypotheses are proven false or their model fails to match expectations.

New School Approaches Lead to Success

To improve student success after graduation, colleges must involve students in team activities. This means moving beyond the lecture hall, classroom and library to embrace events and competitions as educational technologies. In particular, Meetups, Jams, Hackathons and eSports afford students opportunities to develop their skills and talents on many levels. In these events, students form teams with others and, by chance and sometimes by design, use their own wits and ingenuity to adapt to challenging circumstances. Each deserves consideration when constructing New School learning environments.

Meetups

The only real difference between a college class session and a meetup is that only enrolled students attend classes. If an existing college chooses to open some class sessions to outsiders, there are powerful mechanisms available for doing so. The Meetup.com portal[81] currently helps thousands of meetups occur each week, bringing millions together "to do, explore, teach and learn the things that help them come alive". With some encouragement from faculty, students can attract professionals to campus by holding their own meetups. More advanced students regularly attend local meetups in their areas of interest as a matter of course. Enterprising students have found that virtually anything learned in class can be brought into sharper focus with feedback from professionals who are practicing in the field.

Treating class sessions more like meetups is also made possible as more college course materials are delivered online. The "flipped classroom", a form of blended learning in which students prepare for class using online resources, opens up class time for questions and work on projects. This kind of "class as meetup" provides a structure in which students can form study groups to make sense of assignments from a variety of fresh perspectives.

Jams

Pickup games provide a creative outlet for athletes by simulating competitive events, without official game status. The

---

81 meetup.com posts their volume of activity at https://www.meetup.com/about/

same can be said of jams. When organized as a gathering of talent with expertise in research, writing, design, art and programming, teams can prototype remarkable products in a short period of time. In such a team setting, students participate in the entire product development process, so they are exposed to how their particular interests fit with the talents of others.

Jams feature constraints that help teams focus their efforts. A restricted period of time, from a few hours to a couple of days, intensifies the atmosphere as teams brainstorm a project, research the elements to be included, then design and prototype their entries. In order to enhance the spontaneity of the event, organizers typically withhold the theme (what is to be built) until shortly before the jam begins. Doing this in a college environment helps faculty focus attention on specific learning objectives. As an example, Cogswell's Global Game Jam event[82] attracted 32 participants from industry as well as the student body. That event resulted in 8 teams producing game prototypes within a 48 hour period over a weekend.

Hackathons

Perhaps no recent pedagogical method has taken root so deeply in colleges as the hackathon.[83] More structured than a jam, hackathons are structured in phases, with specific outcomes, judging and prizes for winners. Each phase emphasizes skills that might not be well developed by all members of a team, so they must "cut and fill" for each other, using the resources

82 Cogswell's GGJ site provides a portfolio of completed projects at http://globalgamejam. org/2017/jam-sites/cogswell-college/games

83 Hackathon Pedagogies as Educational Technology: http://venturewell.org/open2014/ wp-content/uploads/2013/10/DUHRING.pdf

available to them at the event.

Since the purpose of the event is known in advance, some teams prepare in advance, often with hopes of recruiting the talent they need to field a winning entry. The outstanding trait of a successful team is the intensity and cohesiveness they develop as they work together toward their goal and final presentation. A balanced set of skills across the team, from pitching the project in order to attract talent, to developing the project concept, and then to producing the prototype and presenting the project to judges. Students who go from one hackathon to the next have an opportunity to refine their concepts and make major improvements with each event.

Colleges are supporting their students by recognizing hackathon projects in class. By building campus locations that feel like studios, they encourage students to experiment with ideas, pitch projects to each other and build prototypes that might be useful in competition. They know venture capitalists and hiring managers value what students build together as much as what classes they take. "Students need this kind of space all the time, not just at hackathons," says Stacey Sickels Locke, senior director of development at the University of Maryland, which is building a lab for engineering students to experiment with virtual reality hardware and software.

Students and Startups

For students, the hidden value of startups is that they will network with others. For example, walking into an established business, say, a bank, follows tightly prescribed conversations. Students who are curious about how the bank operates, about what kind of jobs people do at the bank, will probably find out more by talking to a banker at a party than walking into a bank and asking. Walking into a startup means entering an environment where everyone in the enterprise is constantly practicing their story, providing updates, and asking questions for feedback on new initiatives.

Many institutions of higher education are adapting to embrace their local ecosystems. New School-focused colleges are building partnerships and co-working spaces so students have the opportunity to meet professionals and pursue meaningful projects.. They invite professionals to speak to their classes, not only about their business but also to give feedback on student projects. Increasingly, the most popular courses on college campuses are projects done with outside participation, which often means weekly Skype calls to set priorities and review accomplishments. And, through these and other activities, students identify hone the talents they need to develop as they grow.

In the process, students benefit from their exposure to fresh new ideas and businesses made possible through opportunities offered by their college or university. The screening mechanism provided by faculty and staff to find good partners stimulates student imaginations. They learn the language of emerging technology. Probably most importantly, they use their exposure to translate what they learn in the classroom to add value when they graduate.

When Projects Become Ventures

Understanding how an idea can be developed into a sustaining venture, of creating something that takes on a life of its own, can be experienced through hands-on, team-oriented processes in college. These projects afford students insights into what it takes to operate as a professional. Whether a student is the driving force behind a venture or a member of a founding team, they sense the value being created- both what they create as a team and through the role they play as individual contributors.

Feasibility and sustainability testing requires real-world feedback. There is no better time than in college for entrepreneurial teams to pitch their ideas, support their hypotheses, and provide metrics for the early traction they have achieved with early customers. This practice also leads to deep learning about culture, history, anthropology and human behavior.

For example, User Experience Design, or UX is a field field didn't exist twenty years ago, yet it is at the root of what makes a venture successful today. The field is part of what is known as HCI, or Human Computer Interaction. During the personal computer revolution of the 1990s, the skills needed to design graphic interfaces to computer programs spawned new careers for non-technical engineers and designers. User testing and screen-oriented interface design and challenged engineers to think deeply about those who use their products. A development team might include a UI expert for every 30 engineers. As computing devices became more ubiquitous and mobile, how users experience technology has blossomed into the field of UX.

Many startups, in particular, practice what is known as "customer development", which tests every idea and prototype they produce early in the development cycle. On such teams, it is not unusual for everyone to be concerned with who is using the technology, and for a UX expert to be included with every 4-5 engineers. There are currently no standard academic paths to UX. The Stanford Institute of Design, or the "d School", might be closest to providing a proving ground, but students often discover important opportunities through the connections they make with professionals outside of college.

Without experience with professionals, whether through hackathons or internships, students may well find themselves on the outside of the forces that are changing how we live. They have to employ higher education on their own, with no school, in order to make the connection. Now learn to do what they love, what they are good at, and what others find valuable. When students actuate their gifts in these ways, they are on their way. By rubbing shoulders with peers and professionals, inspiration can strike in the most unlikely of settings. Teams form organically when imaginations spark, then crystallize as they embark on missions to make things. By participating in making what was once a dream, students become fully engaged in their own learning and adaptation: they experience self-actualization together, the highest motivator in which realizing their full potential takes place.

And so it goes in an increasingly uncertain and chaotic world. Higher education might start in college, but with technology, is generating brand new professions at an astounding rate. In June of 2016, the World Economic Forum published a report simply titled "10 jobs that didn't exist 10 years ago" included the following job opportunities for new talent, each of which requires "new school" higher education:[84]

---

84 10 jobs that didn't exist 10 years ago, https://www.weforum.org/agenda/2016/06/10-jobs-that-didn-t-exist-10-years-ago/

- App Developer
- Social Media Manager
- Driverless Car Engineer
- Cloud Computing Specialist
- Big Data Analyst
- Data Scientist
- Sustainability Manager
- YouTube Content Creator
- Drone Operator
- Millenial Generational Expert

Professionals must continually draw on their ability to observe the world around them deeply, to make sense of what they see, to adapt to the world as it is, to bring out their best and apply it to the situation at hand. Even with no school as a support, the higher education process becomes an essential asset in an ever changing world. "No school" here is about students realigning with their natural ability to learn as a life-long practice. It is about engaging with communities to practice and adapt to changing circumstances. If the focus is on helping students learn how to be curious, collaborate with others, create extraordinary things and in the long run, adapt to this ever-changing world we live in, higher education must be prepared to create an adaptive environment that promotes resiliency.

Still, the calculation of return on investment cannot be left aside. Institutions of higher education have to embrace the jobs that are being invented as well as the academic jobs that foster innovation and research. Faculty and individuals managing startups, by working together, can meld current curricula to generate the kinds of talent that make a difference in the real world.

A new school college experience exposes students to a multitude of new ideas, startups and ventures. They can try on jobs through projects and learn the intrinsic value they can provide. They can try things and fail in a safe learning environment, while under the guidance of faculty, mentors and peers. They actuate, commit to teach each other and to missions, in order to make things happen. They find where their mastery can make a difference, whether as an artist, scholar, scientist or engineer. This is the reason to go to college and it doesn't require going to a prestigious institution. It can be done at a reasonable price and close to home.

Bentley University recently identified tech industry professions that are in need of talent. While many of these jobs require advanced degrees and industry experience, colleges should examine how their curriculum prepares students for them at an undergraduate level.[85]

---

[85] It's Time for the Hybrid Job, http://www.bentley.edu/prepared/2016-jobs-skills-report

Today's Opportunities

These job functions represent over four million jobs that need to be filled at salaries that any college graduate would die for. Typically, there are few or no college degrees or academic programs that exist to feed talent to them. The Bentley PreparedU Report analyzed key jobs and skills across nine job categories representing different business, IT, and analytics functions—such as marketing, HR, and data analysis.

The Bentley University job market analysis was conducted by the job market analytics firm Burning Glass, drawing from the company's detailed database of online employer demand, which includes over 100 million current and historical job postings collected from close to 40,000 online job sites. Using an artificial intelligence engine, Burning Glass extracted information from each unique posting relating to job titles, skill requirements, requested credentials, salary, and the length of time postings remained open. The data was aggregated and analyzed to identify in-demand jobs and skills across key business, IT, and analytics jobs.

Social media, digital journalism and content origination has been turned upside down by technologies from desktop publishing to Instagram. The number of open jobs in this area has more than doubled in a year to over 115,000 job openings currently posted. According to Burning Glass, the average salary of $62,680 in this category surpasses what "traditional" journalism pays at newspapers and magazines. Startups hiring students at entry level wages need the energy of new graduates on their teams. The salaries they offer enable those they hire to pay back their student loans and look forward to more opportunities as they develop their craft.

The area called business development didn't exist thirty years ago. These professionals can come from any academic or professional background but they must understand how a business operates as a whole. To be successful, they must communicate well with empathy for their peers while driving change. Those who have that skillset enjoy an average salary of $80,887, according to Burning Glass. There are currently nearly half a million positions open, an increase of 50% in a year. Recent college graduates must have hands-on experience working with teams in order to move into this field.

Collecting, analyzing and acting on large data sets is now critical to business growth and innovation. As a new field that impacts the very nature of an enterprise, every venture backed company is looking to improve their business through the data that it generates. The field values asking the right questions and structuring perspectives from rivers of information provided by billions of discrete events, then devising mechanisms to automate the process to deliver insights in the right time and place so actions can be taken. With Burning Glass reporting nearly 300,000 jobs open in the area and an average salary of $76,384, recent college graduates can dive right in if they work well in team settings. They will come up to speed through meetups and internships to apply what they have learned.

Databases have broken into applied specialties around platforms like SAP, Oracle and NoSQL. The combined disciplines for these alone are seeking over 1.5 million new hires. Burning Glass says they pay average salaries in the $90,000 range.

Mathematics is also in great demand. Everything that needs to be modeled and manipulated can benefit from tools build with effective algorithms. Mathematical minds lend themselves to optimizing systems of all kinds. There are over quarter of a million jobs to be filled in this area, paying average salaries of over $70,000, according to Burning Glass.

Sales no longer means pushing products and doing deals. Jobs can be in Developer Relations and Partner Development. These indirect selling methods are growing fast. Burning Glass reports there are over 800,000 open jobs featuring average salaries of $70,470.

Venture backed companies are now looking for decision-making, collaboration, mentoring and process improvement skills among those they seek to employ. These terms represent what companies are looking for, even if they don't define a specific job. People with these skills can move from one side of an organization to another. Combined, Burning

Glass says they represent over 850,000 current job openings with average salaries over $80,000.

Higher Education as a Process

We must think of higher education as a process, not a place. It is a mechanism for students to learn how to learn and accomplish many things. It requires skills for seeing and reading observationally, for gathering and structuring data and other inputs, and for making sense of things as part of a group and individually. Applying these skills properly enables students to commit wholeheartedly to plans of action and to experience positive results beyond college.

Students grow with proper guidance within carefully constructed opportunities in college. Once they have moved into their careers, students invoke and refine their higher education skills in order to adapt to a world as it changes around them. For many, it will become a fundamental part of who they are. They become more resilient, more likely to adapt to change and to work in team situations complimenting other skillsets.

College, then, is an incubator for learning. The skills needed for higher education must be put in place and practiced. These are not mere concepts. They have to be experienced and implemented to take root and grow. A safe environment for individual exploration must be provided. Mixing freely with peers and mentors, students find their footing as they give voice to their own unique perspectives. College is a time to refine purpose through experimentation, finding the intersection of personal gifts, individual preferences and what is needed in the world.

A White-water World

Preparing students for the world as professionals no longer consists of specialists doing only what they were trained to do. Duhigg writes, "A worker today might start the morning by collaborating with a team of engineers, then send emails to colleagues marketing a new brand, then jump on a conference call planning an entirely new line of business while also juggling team meetings with accounting and the party-planning committee."

College administrators and faculty can look to industry to appreciate what needs to be done. No longer does a degree within a discipline define a career path. Working across disciplines requires a set of skills many of today's colleges are not designed to develop. Shifting from grading individuals to evaluating teams will uproot everything. Yet, if team success is what matters most, then students must learn to make themselves essential while at school. Self-actualization is well within the capacity of college students. The technology and pedagogies afforded students today promise an elite higher education at every institution.

We are at a tipping point, a major shift. Students want guidance, not lectures. They need skills, coaching and mentoring. The need opportunities to work together on projects in teams. They have technical resources at their fingertips and know how to use them. Most of all, they must be prepared to function effectively on their own once they have left their school days behind. By turning to each other, by working on teams with the resources at their disposal, they can commit themselves to making their own futures, of finding their own paths in life.

Lifelong Learning and Adaptation

At an individual level, the higher education process repeats itself throughout a lifetime. College represents a first time through the cycle of adaptation and the transformation that comes with it. The process of learning how to learn is often cited by graduates as their most relevant college outcome. As graduates move through their careers, as they evolve as a neophyte trainee, an expert, a master and a mentor, they repeat what they practiced in college and adapt their practices to the situations they face.

The tinkering they had the opportunity to do in school is as important as the knowledge they acquired along the way. In other words, what they "made" in school is as important as their degrees. How they employed their own skills and knowledge while in college is what hiring managers are looking for. In many hiring situations, a college degree is required, yet a portfolio is what helps students land a job. Students must be able to point to projects they were involved with and must be able to describe their role and how they handled the challenges faced by their team.

Strategically, the mission of higher education can be fulfilled with more attention paid to student learning by doing, as evidenced by their adaptations. How students join teams, create meaningful projects and step into roles is critical to the new educational processes that are well within the capability of any college or university. The general acceptance and legitimacy provided by a college degree will continue to reflect a valuable credential and send a unique cultural message that identifies its holder as someone worthy of respect and consideration. The quest for degree attainment will not go away but will need to be supported by real world evidence of accomplishment to retain value.

The End of Lecturing, the Beginning of Storytelling

For centuries, the lecture has stood as the foundation of the higher educational experience. Everyone loves a good storyteller, as evidenced by the popularity of TED Talks. However, at its worse, Nobel laureate Carl Wieman, a professor at Stanford, equates the college lecture with the antiquated medical practice of bloodletting. For centuries, cleansing the body by the withdrawal of blood was thought to be the best way to prevent illness and disease. The British Science museum claims it was the primary practice of surgeons until the 1800s.[86] Wieman says the practice of college lectures is long overdue for an overhaul. The research data he has amassed shows that students retain very little of what is presented to

---

86 Bloodletting, http://www.sciencemuseum.org.uk/broughttolife/techniques/bloodletting

them even in top notch universities.[87] So, he has been teaching in a new way. He has students discuss a problem in small groups. He observes them struggle to make sense of things on their own. In this "active learning" approach, students must figure out what is important and what is not. He says, "The learning is happening as the students are figuring things out. I have data to back it up." Through this method, his failure rate has gone down and students grades have gone up.

Research measuring learning in hands-on, team oriented activities shows great promise. Stanford's Paulo Blikstein has been developing measurement techniques by tracking student movements while working on projects. Using low-cost Kinect sensors, his team gathers data on postures. Students engaged in tasks lean forward with both of their hands on the table. When they sit upright and manipulate things with just one hand, they are semi-active, toying the possibilities. At times, they become passive and reflective, leaning back and letting their imaginations guide them.

Blikstein evaluated these postures across the worst, average and best students. Not surprisingly, the best students move between these three postures most fluidly, spending almost an equal amount of time focused on task-oriented activity, playing with alternatives and reflecting on what they have observed.[88]

His research also measures interaction of team members on group projects. Traditional testing forces students into individual silos. By working with groups of peers, students learn

87 A Nobel Laureate's Education Plea: Revolutionize Teaching, http://www.npr.org/sections/ed/2016/04/14/465729968/a-nobel-laureates-education-plea-revolutionize-teaching

88 Unraveling Students' Interaction Around a Tangible Interface Using Multimodal Learning Analytics, http://blog.bertrandschneider.com/wp-content/uploads/2012/01/23_102-844-3-CE.pdf

to unpack complexity in order to find meaning. They decode how they see the world more rapidly through the perspectives of others. Rather than accepting the point of view of a single authority, they are better informed by gathering inputs from several sources and taking it from there.[89] In the process, students develop an awareness of their own beliefs. They deconstruct them into their essential elements and create their own authenticity from there.

"We had students working in pairs on maker activities. We identified one as the "driver" of the activity—in control of the computer, the keyboard, etc.—and the other as the passenger", Blikstein told EdSurge.[90] "When we had a pair of two high GPA students, of course they performed well. When we had a pair of low GPA students, they tended not to perform well. But when we paired a high GPA student with a low GPA student, and mixed up the roles driver and passenger, we found something unexpected. The groups that had the low GPA student as the driver performed almost as well as the groups of two high GPA students. The message to teachers is: when you are creating groups in a makerspace, try having the "weaker" student be in control of the computer, Legos, robotic kit, etc. with the help of a "stronger" student."

89 Aaron Cohn tutoring, https://www.youtube.com/watch?v=wKd922oDtUU

90 Stanford FabLearn's Paulo Blikstein On the Efficacy of Maker Ed: It's About Process, Not Products, https://www.edsurge.com/news/2016-05-26-stanford-fablearn-s-paulo-blikstein-on-the-efficacy-of-maker-ed-it-s-about-process-not-products

Anatomy of a Storyteller

Stories make a difference and good storytellers make an impact in classrooms. Colleges that provide environments to network, play and study in enriched classrooms are teaching adaptation skills. Even lectures can have value when disguised as play. The late University of California, Berkeley professor Marian Diamond, an excellent new school example, provided one of the first YouTube series of lectures for her Integrative Biology 131 class in 2005. Her first lecture[91] introduces students to the course and also reveals how she teaches and why she operates as she does. Note she is sketching out the course for her students, and within her lecture she has them sketch their notes along with her—she has them mimic her actions.

---

91 Integrative Biology 131 - Lecture 01: Organization of Body, https://www.youtube.com/watch?v=S9WtBRNydso

Even with 750 students in her class, she knows from decades of experience and a deep passion for her role exactly what they need to do to quickly absorb the material she presents. She has buried gems throughout her presentation for students to discover. Dr. Diamond makes learning an interactive game.

At the 5:30 mark in the lecture,[92] she tells her audience she wants them to use "kinesthetic sense", to write in their own handwriting exactly what she writes on the board. She is reinforcing learning by asking them to recall what they have just witnessed.

At the 6:41 mark,[93] she requires her audience to introduce themselves to someone they don't know. To ask who they are, what they are studying and what they think they might want to become. She then calls for their attention and speaks to the power of peers. "We consider ourselves a big family here", she says and then she makes arrangements to help students find "study buddies" and at the end, invites two students at random to have lunch with her at the faculty club. Talk about networking and the value of finding alternative perspectives that help students adapt to the rigors of what lies ahead!

At the 15:07 mark, she recommends a coloring book for her course, in order to reinforce the kinesthetic aspects to learning. She mentions that the book was written by a former student and has sold over 4 million copies. [94]

Considering that this video was taken at a time before MOOCs, most online course designers haven't developed effective use of kinesthetic methods to embed this kind of learning experience through their platforms. After all, here it is

---

92 Ibid, https://www.youtube.com/watch?v=S9WtBRNydso&feature=youtu.be&t=5m30s
93 Ibid, https://www.youtube.com/watch?v=S9WtBRNydso&feature=youtu.be&t=6m41s
94 Ibid, https://www.youtube.com/watch?v=S9WtBRNydso&feature=youtu.be&t=15m7s

clearly a core aspect of traditional elite-level higher education and one that encourages present and future adaptability.

At the 29:22 mark, she explains why she writes in front of the class, "because it gives you time to think." This reflection process ends up taking a substantial amount of class time. When watching the lecture, the observer can almost sense the students considering what they are observing as she writes on the board.[95] Of course, she is prodding her students to take control of their own learning, to let their curiosity guide them as she patiently documents the course in front of them.

Finally, at the 42:24 mark,[96] she expands on the "art of science" with a view from a scanning microscope inside a bone. She then shares a fascinating image cut through a skull and another generated by an MRI device. She asks her students to reflect on their own image when they next look at themselves in the mirror, to imagine the structures in play as they move their awareness, to see themselves in a new way.

Reflecting on this experience, without question, Professor Diamond is sketching a fascinating new world for her audience. She is an artist, as are all great teachers. This master of the art of the story offers her students a new way of seeing themselves. She knows this will force them to reconsider how they think, even to think deeply for themselves often for the first time.

She knows that higher education is not what she is doing, it is what is happening to her students. She inspires and prods them to adapt, and to compose themselves in the process. This classic introduction to anatomy provides a foundational understanding of how learning starts with a sketch, a hint of what

95 Ibid, https://www.youtube.com/watch?v=S9WtBRNydso&feature=youtu.be&t=29m22s
96 Ibid, https://www.youtube.com/watch?v=S9WtBRNydso&feature=youtu.be&t=42m24s

might be developed further.

Professor Diamond's methods are not unlike those employed by the engineer who sketches his process flow on a whiteboard so his contractors can apply their skills correctly, the entrepreneur who sketches his financial model on the back of a napkin so a potential employee or investor is moved to get involved, or the manager who sketches the timeline of a project so her team understands their role in the process.

Professor Diamond mentions a one-unit extension course in which professionals from various careers provide brief sketches of their lives and how they now apply what they have learned beyond college. She sets the stage for her students to become their own teachers and to pursue their own higher education, their own art. In short, she is teaching them how to prepare themselves for the future.

Play In Higher Education

In 1985, Nobel Laureate Paul Berg was frustrated that university students were studying about DNA in textbooks rather than experimenting in labs. "Wet labs" require test tubes, expensive machinery and chemicals, yet they enable the kind of play, exploration and experimentation that enables adaptation and learning.

These laboratory functions were too complex to simulate on the personal computers of the day, but Berg was able to inspire Steve Jobs to focus his NeXT computer company on education and to develop simulations. Not surprisingly, when seen in retrospect, Steve Jobs purchased Pixar at about the same time. We can only imagine that he was thinking about college students interacting with animations as deeply as the BLAM lab now works with stroke victims.

As reported by the New York Times in 1987, "'People learn best by being in a learning environment, which means that ideally, you'd offer a physics student a personal linear accelerator, or a ride on a train going the speed of light," Mr. Jobs said in a 1986 speech. "You'd take a biochemistry student and let him experiment in a $5 million DNA wetlab. You'd send a student of 17th century history back to the time of Louis XIV." Obviously time travel is not practical or possible but it forces us to think about the possibilities of hands-on experiential learning opportunities.[97]

It's more than 25 years later now, and the challenge in education is no longer about the technology. All that Steve Jobs envisioned and more, is readily available using smartphones, networks, Internet services and soon, virtual reality.

How students establish control over the technology and apply it to their own desires holds more promise than ever before. Their notebooks, code repositories, websites and collaborative ventures show what they have made, what they have learned, and give us insight into the world they are stepping into. It is proof of their learning and the achievement they have demonstrated.

In his classic TED talk, Sugata Mitra describes "self organized learning environments" as being the future of education.[98] He brilliantly describes the origins of schools, distinguished by rows of desks and students doing exactly the same work alongside each other without talking. These schools came about at a time when the systems used to rule the British Empire required ledger books to be transferred around the globe by ship.

---

97 Can Steve Jobs Do It Again? http://www.nytimes.com/1987/11/08/business/can-steve-jobs-do-it-again.html
98 Sugata Mitra, https://www.ted.com/speakers/sugata_mitra

The innovation of the time was a world-wide bureaucratic computer, powered by human calculators, that was put in place to manage the global enterprise. Schools were designed to provide workers who could be just as effective in New Zealand as in Canada. Mitra exclaims that this system works well to this day.

The problem is, it was designed for a world that no longer exists. His "school in the cloud" project is focused on creating a new system based on how students learn. A system in which encouragement, curiosity and peer interests spark adaptation and growth.

A growing body of learners and post-graduates around the globe are creating their own learning environments. Co-working spaces have sprung up to help career changers, down-shifters and entrepreneurs to foster their ideas, form teams and try out new approaches. This is a concept that is easily implemented on many college campuses.

One example is the Hacker Dojo in Silicon Valley, which thinks of itself as a kind of college. The people that make up the Dojo community are what make it special. Members pay a fee to join, almost like a new kind of country club, and benefit from the opportunities provided by what other members are working on.

Similar co-working spaces are springing up around the globe. They encourage mixing, exploring and creativity. Members value the benefit of associating with others who are focusing on their strengths, who figure out what motivates them, what gets them out of bed in the morning. They help each other walk through ideas to surface actionable choices. They test out new ventures. Some work at their "day job" while they play with side projects on evenings and weekends. The freedom they feel, to "go anywhere from here", might be summed up by those who say, "One day, your life will flash before your eyes-make sure it is worth watching!"

Enriched environments that eliminate feelings of isolation and facilitate movement, play and exploration increasingly exist in high-tech companies. These open, studio- style offices invite walking meetings, show-and-tell presentations, the formation of missions and the recruitment of teams to execute them.

Bringing movement into the workplace or classroom encourages alliances. It fosters interactions where workers and students speak of their own experience in ways they never would in a formal "meeting" atmosphere. Their sense of identity and purpose can develop from the feedback of their peers, not merely the expectations of their roles.

As an example, Facebook's new Seattle offices will feature a rooftop park-like setting with walking trails and breath-taking vistas, as well as stadium seating inside for larger meetings.[99] Increasingly, new industrial environments are designed to feel like college campuses! The nature of work being done in many industries requires innovation, and employees must act as much like students as they also adapt to a world of continual change.

When colleges provide students the opportunity to interact in these sorts of environments, they form alliances that can last a lifetime. When they embark on projects together, they can explore their interests and hone their strengths. They identify their own passions as well as the roles they are called upon to

---

99 Sneak Peek: Facebook plans epic rooftop park, with walking trails and giant fire pit, at new Seattle office, http://www.geekwire.com/2015/sneak-peek-facebook-plans-epic-roof-top-park-with-walking-trails-and-giant-fire-pit-at-new-seattle-office/

fill. Above all else, they develop an ethic through their efforts. They become "mission-ready" through their own activity, through the roles they play and the projects they participate in.

Steve Jobs spoke of making the world a better place, of making a dent in the universe. To do that, he had to ask where he and his company fit in this world. "What we are about isn't about making boxes for people to get their jobs done, although we do that well", he said in 1997, shortly after returning to Apple after it acquired NeXT. "Apple's core value is that we believe that people with passion can change the world for the better."[100]

In an Apple message to teachers from 1997, Jobs said, "Some people think that the primary use of technology in schools is rote learning, drill and practice, so kids are prepared for the tests they take in school. But that's not why we are all here. We are here to teach these kids how to learn, how to preserve their magical curiosity and how to express themselves creatively.

"In business, the people that get ahead are not the people that know the facts. The people that get ahead are the people who know how to get the facts, and who know how to get insight into them and how to creatively express that insight...to sell the rest of their colleagues and eventually their customers."[101]

This expression of what higher education means- to gather data through a keen awareness of who to model and who to listen to, to make sense of the data with others in such a manner as to act with purpose and commitment- took even someone like Steve Jobs, a true visionary, years to develop.

---

100 Best marketing strategy ever. Steve Jobs Think different / Crazy ones speech, https://www.youtube.com/watch?v=keCwRdbwNQY
101 Steve Jobs talking about education, https://www.youtube.com/watch?v=zo23bx2v99k

It suggests a new model for colleges and universities that centers around undergraduate student learning. At a time in their lives when their bodies and minds are adapting to everything around them, surrounding these students with peers and mentors, enabling them to move and create in order to experience their own abilities and to find their own place, their own voice, this is the value of higher education. This is the beginning of a four-year cycle (more or less), in which they will experience their own resilience and adaptability.

Putting it All Together

Students are surrounded by new environments and new role models. They choose who to listen to, whether faculty or peers. They seek out inspiration and companions. In well-designed courses, students learn to express themselves not only with groups of friends but also within the structures of the compositions they create. The presentation by Dr. Diamond illustrates how classroom activities powerfully influence what students experience.

Traditionally, composition is thought of as linked to writing assignments. Using letters to form words to form scenarios that form compositions made up of characters and actions has been the mainstay of traditional higher education. Ultimately, students learn to tell stories through these kinds of compositions, to express themselves, to persuade, to engage through the practice of putting words on paper.

The patience required to move from the rudiments of sentence structure through to building essays that prove a point or tell a story taxes even the most talented student. Although increasingly this is a skill set that employers are seeking.

As we have seen, employing group activities, mimicry, and art enables compositions to bubble up ad hoc. The notebooks of Professor Diamond's students form the testimony to prove the value of creating sketches. Her performance is not a listening and thinking exercise, it is not about consuming knowledge. It is about mimicry, about networking, about learning to perform and to produce. Adapting to the world like this is what makes good college courses special.

The effect of a lecture presented this way, as a sketch for students to elaborate on in their own way, helps each of them discover their own talents, to think critically about their own path. Creating sketches that evolve into compositions capable of persuading, engaging and informing takes years of practice, feedback and inspiration.

Colleges and any new form of higher education must confront the issues raised here. Students, as suggested by centuries of teachings, learn from direct observation, from making sense of the things they observe and by rendering out new versions of themselves along with their work. By embracing such a view of higher education, we can develop effective new methods to engage more students and to address the issues we now face.

Using high tech is no longer for techies alone. Growing industries are eager to employ those equipped with the right tools to participate in essential services- in transportation, health care, housing, food/water supply and government. These tools and needs must be embraced and harnessed throughout the college experience.

The current mismatch of students with college degrees but no job opportunities has created massive non-traditional educational alternatives for learning the skills that employers are looking for. Of these, online coding academies and immersive technology boot camps have sprung to prominence both on-ground and online. Their typical student is a working adult who has already received a college degree. This kind of student wants to transition into growing industries, either while working (in the case of online courses) or by immersing themselves for a short period (one week or less).

Recently, the Department of Education has sought to couple non- traditional higher educational programs with regionally accredited degree-granting academic institutions to acknowledge how education is changing and being offered outside the walls of college institutions. It's too early to tell if the "Experimental Sites" initiative will take hold, but it demonstrates the level of adaptation that colleges now face.[102] Which colleges will partner with non-academic training organizations to prepare people for high demand technology jobs? And what will those arrangements look like? Who will they benefit? How will it affect the traditional student out of high school? Will they feel the need to go through four years of college or will they opt out for a more direct path to a good job? All of these are questions institutions will need to answer and perhaps accommodate.

What we think we know is that the transition from personal life to professional life takes time for students right out of high

---

[102] Notice Inviting Postsecondary Educational Institutions To Participate in Experiments Under the Experimental Sites Initiative; Federal Student Financial Assistance Programs Under Title IV of the Higher Education Act of 1965, as Amended https://federalregister.gov/a/2015-26239

school. Newer more direct paths are yet to be tested. Establishing a safe space and providing inspiration through faculty and community has always been thought to set in motion personal transformations and much more. It is why we believe there is still an important reason for college.

The meaningful application of their capabilities deserves to be the centerpiece of their college experience. Shifting how we view higher education starts with understanding that "...getting into college or being at college are not the marks of people who are smart. They are part of a person striving to become more accomplished."[103]

The college process, then, supports adaptation by deepening a student's capabilities while expanding their capacity to perform. Colleges increasingly find they must prepare students to compete effectively against older graduates emerging from boot camps, online nanodegrees and other alternatives to college.

Using This Book

The authors hope that you have picked up some ideas for how to be a new school college or university if you are an administrator or faculty member. If you are a parent or student, the choice is yours. Make your education count and trust that the single most important thing you can learn in college is adaptability that will prepare you for the future as the environment continues to change in ways we cannot even predict. We wish you all the best as you make your decision to join the new school vision.

---

103 Dear High School Seniors, Applying to College is the Easy Part, http:// www.thedaily-beast.com/articles/2015/11/01/dear-high-school-seniors-applying-to-college-is-the- easy-part.html

APPENDIX:
Game Studio–An Unconventional Game Design and Development Course

To the casual observer, Jerome Solomon's Game Studio class—a game design and development course—at Cogswell College might present an unremarkable first impression. When walking into the class, one sees 25 students at their workstations. An alert visitor might first note how the room is quiet and yet active at the same time. Looking closer, they might notice that each student is working on something unique. They are using different tools to do different things, all at the same time. Some are working in code, whether C sharp or Python. Others are working in Maya or Photoshop. Still others are deep into a spreadsheet or word processor. More interestingly, students regularly get up and walk over to their colleagues to hold mini-conferences to resolve questions as they come up. What's going on?

Key Takeaways from the Game Design and Development Course

"The goal of our Game Studio class is to put students in an industry style production studio", says Jerome Solomon, Dean of the College. "Students are grouped into functional teams in order to build a working game for a client like AC Transit within a two semester time period. They use industry standard game design tools for version control and team communications as well as for game development and production. In addition, they must interact with each other to design and develop a working game product, provide updates to our client and receive feedback every step of the way." As an upper division college game design and development course, Game Studio has helped Cogswell's game program achieve a Top 20 ranking from Princeton Review in 2016. Alumni from this program have landed positions at established companies like Google, Accenture, and 2K Games.

Working with a client like AC Transit, students in this game design and development class learn to pitch their ideas and receive feedback on a regular basis. The class is frequently broken into teams to prepare presentations or updates. Advanced students earn team leadership roles: for game design and UI, audio, engineering, art and project management. "I get a strong sense that I'm developing the problem-solving skills that will carry me forward through my industry career", said Sean Langhi, an engineering lead on an earlier Game Studio project who was later hired by Google.

A Course That Turns Thoughts into Things

Students take on responsibilities in this game design and development class related to their abilities and the needs of the team. They learn the process of agile development, of scrums and sprints, while they conceptualize and prototype a game in one semester, then develop and release the game in the next. "I pretty much have to interact with just about everybody," said design lead Jacob Levine. "Every day I spend my time designing new game features or game play mechanics, even evaluating camera angles to determine what will be the best UI." Another game designer, Mohammed Zaid Shaikh developed the idea of progressive generation, where an AC Transit bus will drive through an endless cityscape with new buildings and roadway appearing automatically as a series of tiled 3D objects. "As the bus is moving, the tiles will randomly spawn. I made those tiles."[104]

In a game studio environment such as this, students do what they came to learn. The high degree of coordination across functional game design and development groups in the class enables them to dive into problems as they come up. Cory Binkerd is on the UI team and found himself rigging the foot of a three dimensional human character to enable it to move within the game. "Normally you would do this by parenting one joint to another joint, but in Maya, you have to create a handle that attaches to the first joint and then the second one in order for them to move correctly. Someone figured this out way before me and posted their solution on youtube so I don't have to figure it out on my own." Cory also happens to be colorblind, so the team decided to take that into account. Engineer Christian Saario used Python to create a gray scale script for the artists so they can work in grayscale to ensure that the game works for colorblind people.

---

104 The early project prototype illustrates this tiling functionality along with rough audio and user controls. https://www.youtube.com/watch?v=a29xXSQv8zY

A Culture of Practice in the Class

"This class enforces doing things the right way", said Cody Wright, a member of the art team. "If you do things the wrong way, you have to go back and fix it and that takes up a lot of time." The entire class learns what moves the project forward, and what they can do in their own role. With a UI/Design team of three students, nine engineers, five digital artists and three on the sound team, the team structure enables students to figure things out as they go.

Says Jerome Solomon, "We have some students who are more senior and some are less experienced. The games that we typically try to create in Game Studio go across many different facets of our game design and development curriculum. They really learn to depend on each other."

Assessing Proficiency, Teamwork and Purpose

A simple measure of output reveals a secret strength of the Game Studio class. Over a two-semester cycle, students will check-in over ten thousand individual pieces of code, artwork or other documentation. That pace equates to roughly 3 commits to the version control system every class hour for every student. With so many more data points at his disposal when compared to a more traditional college environment with weekly assignments, rubrics for evaluating performance can be quite nuanced and helpful to student success.

Separate grading rubrics for engineers and artists help drill down to expose three dimensions in which students can excel: technical proficiency, emotional intelligence and personal integrity. These map nicely to the professional world where hiring managers choose candidates who are strong in at least one area, recognizing that some technical superstars can be difficult to work with, some skilled communicators may lack technical chops and some people just make others work better around them. With many opportunities to contribute to the class, students feel empowered and tend to commit themselves more fully.

Bugi Kaigwa led the art team on an earlier project and now works in a similar team environment at 2 K Games. When reflecting on his experience in the class, he said, "Game Studio was a great opportunity for me because I got to work with many different people with different skill sets and different temperaments. Learning how to function in an efficient team was a learning experience for me and relates directly to what I am doing now."

APPENDIX:
Rendering Project X- Alumni Share Their Stories

How does working on a full scale production feel? Is it like the real thing, or does it feel like just another class? Nothing in Project X at Cogswell College is previously produced. Everything, from sound to story to special effects, is generated by students. The process of design, composition and technical execution, when held to professional standards, sets students up for smoothly transitioning into their post graduate careers, and also renders them, in the words on one participant "more social, able to build really strong bonds with everyone, which is very much the atmosphere at creative studios."

Steven Chitwood, class of 2015 and working at Disney Animation, described rendering this way, "Rendering is the process of calculating a final image from a computer. It's the last step that lets you can see what you see on the screen. It requires a lot of computational power to make it so." He was speaking to members of the community who had gathered recently for a private screening of "Trouble Brewing", the latest Project X short animated feature that is now being shown at film festivals. The event featured a panel discussion[105] among 10 alumni who had worked on the project over the past 2-3 years. How they quite naturally shared the stage and the spotlight between them, illustrated what they have learned in the way of developing deep working relations. Sentences often started with a thought and someone else would elaborate or refine it, rendering a most enjoyable evening for all.

A Creative Adventure

The panel was asked just how long it took the farm of render machines to compute the values for a single frame during

105 Project X Premiere Event Q&A- Trouble Brewing, https://www.youtube.com/watch?v=e7EQqP9LArw&feature=youtu.be&t=15m7s

the final stages of production (keep in mind that each frame is 1/24th of a second in duration and the final product is over 400 seconds in length, or over 10,000 frames to be rendered for the entire film). Vineet Vijaykumar, class of '16 and now at Method Studios, estimated the time required to calculate a single frame of the Troll character, once his skin and clothing was textured and lights were put on the scene, took about 40 minutes. "And the environment in the scene was another 30 minutes as well. And if it didn't turn out the way you wanted it, you had to do it again. And, you had to find out what was wrong with it before you could do it again!"

For all Project X teams, students are selected to participate in the development and production of an animated short feature based on their coursework, skills and abilities to work on a project over an extended period of time. As the project evolves, so does the makeup of the Project X team, with each semester bringing in a slightly different set of skills and personalities.

The origins of "Trouble Brewing" were established with guidance from faculty to produce something with goats and a troll, with a theme of a character that acts out and learns that their actions have an impact on others. A small writing team assembled to develop the concepts and illustrate them in storyboard form. This first stage of the project produced a final storyboard for the project in the first 6 weeks. From there, teams of technical engineers and artists created digital models, developed motion systems for them and animated them to bring the story to life. Backgrounds, objects and sounds were designed flesh out the experience. Finally, textures were applied to surfaces, lights were cast and elements in scenes were composited together prior to rendering finished frames.

For students taking a full course load, Project X required long hours. "I just brought my computer in from home and blasted away", said Steve Chitwood. "I tried to stay in the project room as much as I could. It was definitely a good work load but well worth it." Jason Bursese, '15 and now at Kabam Games said, "On the audio side of the production it was long hours. Here we were, full time students and this was another job on top of it." "That's exactly what it was", said Richard Ash, class of '15 and now at Avisys, "The caliber of work that was being done in the audio classes was already high, and we were always trying to do better. We were always pushing ourselves to perform at as high a level as we could."

Team Bonds

"We always had teamwork" added Kristal Sana, class of '15 and now at Blur Studios. "It was very similar to how it works in the industry. You have a team lead, you have supervisors and directors, both students and faculty. It's a learning curve with teammates. We didn't have to rely only on ourselves. I learned from people here on the panel and I am grateful." Added Vineet, "The project environment is different from classes. We wasn't the case where you get an assignment for a week and then it's due and you get graded. Here it was an iterative process. My role was in compositing, so I would start with rendered frames and then ask what was the color or tone or mood we are looking for with a shot. Then I would work on it and show it for feedback on a Tuesday. I'd them go back and work on it some more and show it on Thursday. That back and forth enabled me to do things, sometimes by accident, which turned out really nicely. I enjoyed Project X. It felt like having fun and at the same time working and trying to create something that is really beautiful."

Kegan Chau, class of '15 and now at Hangar 13, a subsidiary of 2K Games, said, "There is a difference between working on a project and balancing your classwork in college. Now, I am asked to focus on a single project at work for a prolonged amount of time. It's a different mindset- it's not like the more you push, the faster it will get out." Jamil Green, class of '14 and now at Apple, said, "I modeled the character of the Troll in "Trouble Brewing", but I had to overcome doubt as I started my career. I can be very intimidating. When you see actual job listings, you look at all the requirements and they are looking for years of experience. At my current position, I applied for the job a year before I got the offer. So, that is one thing that I'll suggest to students coming out of college. If there is a job role that you want, don't be afraid to apply for it. It might come in handy just when you need it. Because, for me, it actually did."

In an evening that felt like campers sitting around the bonfire after dinner, the panel encouraged students to get involved with projects early and often, to meet professionals at conferences and to reach out to recruiters on LinkedIn. Steve Chitwood advised, "In the industry, they want to hear that you know how to collaborate on a team. You're going to do that on the job. You don't want to be an awkward guy, because when a problem arises, you need to communicate." And Steve Mortensen, class of '14 and now working at Crystal Dynamics, dropped what might have been a surprise to many of the students in the audience. He said, "By working on Project X I learned a lot of things that I actually ended up teaching a lot of people at my studio. 'I would say, oh, you guys don't know how to do this?.. it's way faster.. let's do it this way'. Senior guys have been at it for a long time and sometimes don't keep up with the newest pipeline options that Project X gets to explore."

Everyone on the panel smiled knowingly when Vineet said, "My first day on the job I said to myself, 'oh my God, I don't know anything… I have so much to learn'! But the good thing from that is you have that feeling and you are hungry to learn, but at the same time your co-workers know that you are new and they are more than willing to answer your questions. Sometimes it's a little awkward if they are wearing headphones and you have something to ask them! You learn from every-body. I have a pipeline responsibility so I'll learn from different coders, but at the same time I can talk to artists and learn their workflow. I will come away with an understanding, to say 'OK, so this is what we have to do'. Your willingness to learn and the passion that you have is what brings you forward."

POSTSCRIPT:
A Message to High School Students and Their Parents

So much attention is paid to preparing for college as if your higher education is something off in your future. In fact, your higher education should get started while you are still in high school. Your sense of who you are and your purpose in life has already started to form. This sense is formed by a mix of your skills and strengths, what the world needs and what you want to do. Developing your sense of purpose can be done at any time, in any place.

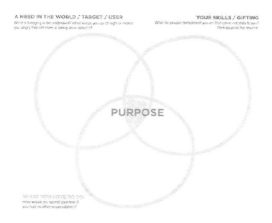

Practice these simple activities on a regular basis and you will note a shift in how you feel, how you approach school and how you look at your future.

Focus on movement. Some of your movements, like a runny nose, are involuntary. Others, like walking or breathing, can be either involuntary or voluntary. In other words, as you think about what you are doing, more of what you do becomes a choice. Imagine skipping a step, walking backwards or taking a different path to the kitchen every so often. Note what choices you make. Observe how it makes you feel to do something different. For example, note where you do something with your right hand (like eating soup with a spoon) and try using your left instead. Note when you are conscious about your movements and when you are not. Note when you are responding and adapting to something in your environment. Use this practice to observe the world around you with fresh eyes. Play with it. Find ways to mix things up and note what changes. If it helps, think of the words spoken by the ancient Greek philosopher Heraclitus. He was famous for his insistence on ever-present change as being the fundamental essence of the universe. He said, "No man ever steps in the same river twice, for it's not the same river and he's not the same man."

Interrogate and speculate. Focus on search in order to form questions. At times, let your imaginations guide you as you move your normal routines. Ask yourself about what you are experiencing, both what you observe around you and how you feel. Start by asking yourself "Why?" questions to frame the movement, to explain what is going on. Then ask "If?" questions to elaborate, to imagine new possibilities. Think about how you would ask these questions to experts. Then, google your questions. Search through pictures, videos, news, maps as well as web sites. Follow related search suggestions and let yourself follow the search paths of others. See where these searches lead you. When you find things that interest you, inquire more deeply. Find out as much as you can with an eye to discovering things you can do with what you have learned. Ask "what if?" to imagine entirely new ways you can see things from a fresh perspective. If you ask the right questions, you discover problems worth thinking about more deeply. These become projects in which you can ask the "How?" questions to break problems into smaller, practical steps. That's right, more movement and more searching.

Show and tell. Have your consciously directed movements and inquiries led to surprises? What evidence has surfaced that support a different perspective than you had before? Tell someone about it. What you have found out about whatever you were searching for helps others understand their own questions. Observe the response you get from friends, family or Facebook. Do they share something similar in return?

You might be surprised how easy it is to deepen friendships this way. Fellow travelers along their own path make fine associates and teammates. Through the practice of sharing what you have learned by presenting the evidence that you have surfaced, others can join you in the process.

By developing your own practice in this way, you choose who to pay attention to and what to observe. Your mindfulness in the process provides you with infinite possibilities, even within constraints of time and circumstance. You choose to keep your approach simple or make it elaborate as you wish. This is the starting point for higher education.

About the Authors

Dr. Deborah Snyder is president of St. Clair County Community College in Port Huron, Michigan and has been in higher education for more than thirty years.

She has worked for several colleges and universities as a professor and more recently in senior academic administration. Dr. Snyder was an early pioneer in Internet-based education and adult learning and has consulted with colleges and universities across the country. She holds a Ph.D in organizational communication, an MBA in marketing, and an undergraduate degree in psychology from Wayne State University, Detroit, Michigan.

John Duhring is the Director of Community Relations for Cogswell College in San Jose, California.

John has been a founding team member at seven startups, generating multiple successful exits. He has applied technology to learning at Prentice-Hall, Apple, Dow Jones and for Stanford's Professional Publishing Courses. A fifth-generation Californian, he received his BS in Business Administration from UC Berkeley.